I0795495

TABLE OF CONTENTS

HOW TO THRIVE AT COLLEGE

MATHILDE ROSS, MD

A GUIDE TO THE UPS & DOWNS OF MENTAL HEALTH ON CAMPUS

DIVERSION BOOKS

Diversion Books
A division of Diversion Publishing Corp.
www.diversionbooks.com

This book is intended for general informational and educational purposes only. It is not a substitute for professional medical advice, diagnosis, or treatment. Readers should always seek the guidance of a qualified health professional with any questions regarding a medical condition or mental health concern. Never disregard professional advice or delay seeking it because of something you have read here.

Diversion Books and colophon are registered trademarks of Diversion Publishing Corp.

For more information, email info@diversionbooks.com

First Diversion Books Edition: April 2026
Trade Paperback ISBN: 979-8-89515-096-2
e-ISBN: 979-8-89515-097-9

Design by Westchester Publishing Services
Cover design by Jonathan Sainsbury // 6x9 design

Printed in the United States of America
1 3 5 7 9 10 8 6 4 2

April—Blunt Forces

May—Graduation Requirements

INTRODUCTION

Recently, I took a day trip with my daughter to New Hampshire for a college visit. During the information session, I received this text (standard typos included): "thinking of you this morning while I am out for a long walk with the dog on Cape Cod I'm halfway through listening to *Anxious Generation* and thinking about our kids can I get your perspective on it?"

This is an ordinary mom/friend in my neighborhood—she hosts a holiday cookie swap every year. She and her husband are highly educated and are raising three teenagers who are at approximately zero risk of having significant mental health problems. Certainly, her kids may one day experience the requisite multi-week funks that come for us all—after a sidelining injury, a broken friendship, a romantic hiccup, a pregnancy scare, etc.—but these kids are well set up for swift recovery and lifelong stability.

She's writing to me because she's been told otherwise.

By media, by well-meaning authors and experts, by just about everyone with a podcast mic, she and so many parents like her have been told to worry, worry a lot, about the next generation.

The kids are NOT all right, the headlines are screaming. And so my friend is doing what good, smart people who research everything do: She is sending me a text in the hope that I can lower her heart rate by telling her what's really going on *and*, at the same time, save her children, *while also* entertaining her with my reassuring (often funny) stories from the trenches.

I can do that. I can do that like crazy.

I have been getting a version of her question just about every day for the past two years, from almost everyone I've ever met. It's a text, an email, a whispered aside, a call. All from parents who are worried about their kids, not because of any concerning behavior they have witnessed, but because of something they have read or heard.

They want to know:

Is there a mental health crisis among youth?

If so, what's causing it?

Are my kids at risk?

My friends with questions know that I am a psychiatrist, aka a medical doctor, who has spent nearly two decades in a cinderblock, ground-floor office at Boston University, counseling young people through the worst of their upheavals (and best of their triumphs).

What these parents may not know—or maybe forgot—is that before I sat in that counseling office with views of idling traffic, I oversaw a psychiatric unit in a hospital across the river. It was my first job out of medical training. I saw a lot. Maybe too much. There, I encountered the depths of human suffering. I learned to recognize the ingredients of a crisis that renders a person unable to safely function in the community. I learned to identify who is at risk.

My first years in the BU counseling office, 2008–2016, were a cakewalk by comparison. I joked with friends that it was ballast to my primary job, raising toddlers. I took to the students. I loved listening to them, their ideas, their creative belief systems. They had problems, for sure—that's a given in my line of work—but also solutions. I came home energized, thrilled to be in proximity to their energy. Their lapses in executive function were a plus, because I could take a catnap during the occasional no-show.

Then, around 2017, came the first uptick in handwringing. This was before the pandemic, when phones and social media, disinformation and climate crisis were "taking over" teenage brains like a deadly fungus.

Then the pandemic. Social distancing. End of days. Another election. Loneliness. Fear.

Put it all in a blender and *whizz*.

My phone has not stopped ringing, since.

So back to my neighbor's question. I have a long answer (this book) and a short one. Both are contrary to so much popular opinion.

The short answer: The kids *are* all right. Not every single one, but the vast majority are very extremely totally all right. The descriptor "anxious generation" is itself a product of anxiety, not reality.

That doesn't mean everything is perfect all the time. These are teenagers, after all. Ergo, there's a new problem every fifteen minutes! It's like waves on the seashore—they just keep coming. But they also keep going away. Waves on the seashore are not a problem; they are part of the ebb and flow of life, especially for young people. A tsunami, on the other hand, is a big, big problem. Luckily, most people know the difference. At least, they used to.

Parents freaking out about how the kids may be freaking out is freaking out the professionals—me and my colleagues—who are trying to help kids figure themselves out. Our clinic volume has approximately doubled during my time at BU. It's a feedback loop of epic proportions that needs an interruption.

I love to interrupt. Not my patients, of course, but everyone else.

How to Thrive at College is my answer to the public confusion on this subject. I invite you into my office to sit with students and hear their stories as I hear them. The patient stories and student experiences described in this book are drawn from real encounters, but identifying details have been altered, combined, or fictionalized to protect privacy. Any resemblance to actual individuals is coincidental, and no case is presented in its entirety. Most represent common scenarios that I have encountered dozens of times.

By taking you behind my office door at BU—as I meet with students over the course of a calendar year—*How to Thrive at College* will:

- Demystify mental health, giving readers the knowledge and agency to parent with less fear.
- Show the major forces that impact the mental health of young people. Some are obvious and some are not; some are downright funny; most are getting no attention in the media.
- Restore confidence for those parents doing it right. If you've been a decent parent for eighteen years, the reward is knowing your adult children can handle whatever life throws at them.

- Give teenagers the knowledge and skills to avoid some of the common pitfalls of young adulthood and develop healthy adult boundaries with their parents.
- Give readers a basic framework for understanding the principles of mental health, so they can understand if the issues getting public attention are fundamental to mental health or peripheral concerns affecting very few.
- Restore joy to the discussion of mental health. This work is fun. Sure, there are terrifying moments, but at a fundamental level, my job is about helping young people reach their potential. Does it get any better than that?
- Nudge the public conversation in a more helpful direction, by increasing understanding and offering pragmatic solutions, as opposed to fanning the flames of anxiety.

That college tour in New Hampshire that I took with my daughter? It went well, thank you for asking. After I received the emergency text from my friend and replied that "the answer required a glass of wine and a few hours," I was able to concentrate on the student docent taking us around. It just so happened that she was an EMT and sometimes responded to on-campus emergencies.

This is my territory!

My hand shot up. My daughter looked up at me pleadingly. I smiled. *It's going to be okay*, I mouthed. But she knew my signals, and she knew where this was going: I was going to get this docent talking, and we were all going to learn things, messy things, about life on this campus!

"Do you get called to emergencies involving fellow students?" I asked.

The docent nodded as I watched my daughter shrink back into the crowd to become someone else's child. I was going to be in for it on the ride home: i.e., the silent treatment, followed by two hours of Taylor Swift, *le plat du jour*.

Still, I persisted: "So, how does that work vis-à-vis privacy, like what if you were called to a friend's apartment?" I couldn't help myself. An EMT student! She was so confident and poised. I was cheering for her as if she were one of my own students, all of them wiser, faster, more resilient than the news and opinionators would give them credit for.

"Well," she began, standing taller. She was the authority among us and knew it. Even my daughter stepped toward her, again, to listen . . .

■ ■ ■

High-achieving families are out of sorts. Conservative, liberal, rich, not rich. They're all tangled up in APs, SATs, ACTs, GREs, test prep, test-optional, $12k private college counselors, 529 plans, and financial aid. They're "keeping up" at any cost, wherever "up" happens to be.

Parents are generally obsessed with their children's success, but in the back of their minds they're wondering, "All this hustling, will it work out? Can we even handle what's coming?" They're hearing about college kids in crisis from every media outlet and their social feeds. They believe in spending money on education *and* stability and happiness, but they're confused about the latter. They want to be those trusted parents whom kids go to in a crisis, but everyone's telling them things have changed, "consult the professionals before it's too late!!!"

The kids are just as confused, wrapping up high school or just starting college. Their lives have been focused on achievement, not development. They understand calculus but never learned how to schedule a haircut. They can perform a solo on stage but can't ask a pharmacist a simple question. They certainly can't make a phone call to a stranger! They think everyone else is perfect, so they pretend to be, too. They're obsessed with politics or apathetic. They're confused about sex but don't want to admit it. They're hanging on their parents' approval but hide it like leprosy.

These dutiful families are all normal, but they don't know it. They need comfort and reassurance and, most of all, information. They're not finding the answers in their media outlets or social feeds—only more questions.

Enter *How to Thrive at College . . .*

This book offers useful information about the mental health side of college life, strategies for communicating about difficult topics, and red flags for identifying when it's the right moment to involve a professional. Parents and teens don't usually read the same books, but this book may be an exception. By writing this as a narrative—memoir woven with advice—rather than pure prescriptive material, I like to think I've found a way to talk to all ages at once. That is what I do in my day job, after all.

If I write myself out of said day job by teaching students how to avoid the pitfalls that land them in my office *and* helping parents understand their role in the lives of their adult children, I'll retire happy.

PREREQUISITES

Before you send your teenager off to college, let's spend a few minutes determining whether they are ready to go. Our society values calendrical age over developmental readiness to an absurd degree. Consider the following: Six weeks before his eighteenth birthday, my son called me because he needed permission to play paintball. This is a young man who would be eligible for the draft in a blink. He drove himself to the paintball facility, paid with money that he earned from his own job, and called his *mother* to sign him in. I did what any reasonable mother would do in this situation: I told him to forge my signature. I trusted him to make a low-stakes decision without parental involvement. (My maternal wisdom was in no way influenced by my desire to have him out of the house for a few hours, or my various challenges with online forms!)

You need a method for determining if your teenager is ready for college that is a little more nuanced than when their eighteenth birthday falls. Consider whether your teenager has experienced the following common milestones:

- failing a driving test, then mustering the courage to take it again
- cutting a finger while cooking or washing dishes and dealing with it
- ruining an entire load of laundry by using the wrong water temperature and admitting it
- remembering a sibling's birthday without being prompted
- pumping gas and paying for it
- winning an argument with you, decisively
- losing an argument with you, decisively

- cooking a meal for the whole family, unassisted
- crying in front of their friends
- dropping everything to support a crying friend
- facing consequences for dropping everything
- working a paid job that they got without a parental connection
- a few crushes
- some sexual exploration
- losing a loved one, including pets, to uncontrollable circumstances
- a trip to the emergency room; full credit for accompanying a friend or sibling
- taking out the trash without being asked
- laughing at themselves

This is a fairly arbitrary, totally representative list. What you're looking for is proof your children have developed life skills, that they bounce back from disappointment and adversity, that they are able to think of others besides themselves, that they are aware of their own folly and that of others, that they can be vulnerable, that they can plan, set priorities, and organize without assistance, that they can assert themselves when required and apologize when wrong. If your teenager hasn't experienced at least half of the rites of passage on this list or demonstrated most of these developmental goals in some other way, there is a good chance they are not ready for college.

Don't panic! Consider this: In nearly two decades of working at a university, I have never met a student who has regretted taking a gap year, or a leave of absence.

The easiest mental health crisis to deal with is the one that never happens. College will still be there when your teenager is ready.

If your teenager is ready for college, that's great—I can't wait to meet them! But I probably won't. Because this book will prepare your family? What I mean is, your teenager is unlikely to meet me because most college students, like most people, will never have any reason to see a psychiatrist.

Need help now?

Just discovered your teenager needs another year before going to college? Or maybe you have a younger teen in the house? There's plenty here for you, too. (If you have mastered the art of parenting teenagers, feel free to skip the **Need help now** interludes. Also, can you give me a call?)

Listen to their music. Get used to it. Learn some lyrics, pick a favorite song, and act excited when it comes on. Whether at home or in the car with the family, you either listen to your teenager's music, or . . . they put their headphones in. Parents, those are your choices. When you live with teenagers, enjoying family conversation with your own music playing is not a thing.

Lemme Go!

Teenagers, do you have any concerns about whether your *parents* are ready for your departure? Here's a screening tool for you:

Do they know the names of all your high school teachers?
Do they still go to all your away games? What about performances: Do they still go to *every single one*, even if you're performing the same number four times in a weekend?
Do they know what book you're reading in English class, or the date of your final exam?
Do they check your grades more often than you do?
Do they still fold your laundry, or take you to get your haircut?
Do you get the impression that all their friends are affiliated with your school or activities?

If you answered *yes* to any of these questions, your parents may be at risk of separation anxiety when you go off to college. Symptoms include texting you several times a day, befriending your roommates' parents, or calling the dean of students multiple times. You have enough to think about without these mortifying scenarios. To help your parents manage the transition, you might recommend that they get a puppy, start gardening, or join a book club.

Consider how much you changed between the ages of ten through fifteen, and how little your parents changed during the same period. Change doesn't come naturally for parents the way it does for kids.

Professionals like me are always encouraging parents of young adults to follow their kids' lead when it comes to negotiating an adult relationship. It helps the process if *you* are able to be clear. The *Lemme Go!* sections are for you, to give some perspective on where parents are coming from, and to help you establish adult boundaries.

PART I

Fall Term—Transition to Adulthood

September—The Basics

CHAPTER ONE

If It's Working, Keep Doing It.

I tumble into my office after being off for the summer. Well, my husband calls my summers "off"; I call my summers "hustling through other essential matters"—like corralling my three children who were also sprung from school—while also fixing broken things that got ignored September through May. I'm somewhere between late and very late, today, because school drop-off for said children was complicated (a child forgot soccer cleats, which is not okay when the child is the daughter of the soccer coach), and I couldn't find parking when I got to BU. Even if I arrived on time, I'd be running behind, because I have forgotten my office login. That's okay, running behind is practically mandatory for doctors, so I feel right back in the role.

By the time I've arranged some new photos, put my lunch in the fridge, and said *hello* to several colleagues I haven't seen since May, my first appointment of the day has already checked in. I take a deep breath, dust off the cobwebs in my brain, and invite him into my office. My body language is meant to project confidence, empathy, and intelligence, while giving absolutely no indication that I may have left the dog without food in her bowl, or that I'm waiting for a callback from a plumber.

This student is having panic attacks. The school year has just begun, and he's having panic attacks almost every day. The heart-pounding-out-of-the-chest, can't-catch-your-breath-think-you're-dying kind. If you've never had one, this is a terrible experience. And this is happening to him a lot.

So his mom told him to make an appointment with our office, and I'm taking a history. No panic attacks before college, and not much anxiety, really, he says.

This can happen, but I'm a little surprised they've gotten so bad, so fast.

I dig a little more and ask about how he spent his time in high school. Cross country and track, he says. I ask how much he was running in high school.

"A lot."

"When was the last time you went running?"

He thinks for a bit. "August, I guess, before I came to school."

So he's gone from too much exercise to none. During the biggest transition in his life, he's not only given up his main outlet, but he's also given up the thing that has structured his time and social life. And he's given it up cold turkey, without giving it much thought.

I tell him to go running. Not like in high school, but regularly. And with friends, if possible. His homework is to go running four to five times per week and come back and see me in two weeks. This is the sort of homework you're likely to get from a psychiatrist who is also a mom and a soccer coach.

About that soccer coaching: A girls' soccer team thrives on the same sort of advice I dole out in my office, though it may not look that way at first blush. My rules are: 1) No cartwheels on the soccer field. All cartwheels must be done off the field, because using your hands is against the rules in soccer; everyone knows that. 2) Crying is okay until it's not. One crying girl is bad luck—it's bound to happen; two crying girls means you better switch to a different activity, because things aren't going well; three crying girls means practice is over, *immediately*, even if practice started five minutes ago. The result: a happy, fuel-efficient team.

Early in my soccer coaching days, one of my girls had a beautiful breakaway toward an open net. Did she score her first goal? Nope, she panicked. Didn't get a shot off. This happened a lot, with several of my players. Balls went wide, got tripped over, or just fizzled. I needed to build my team's confidence, but how? I consulted with more experienced coaches, who told me the obvious (more shooting drills at practice, duh), but my girls needed *confidence*, not just *skills*.

I asked more questions and looked into the rules and . . . I told my girls to dribble the ball straight into the net, instead of taking a shot. This is the sort of instruction you're likely to get from a coach who is also a mom and psychiatrist. It worked! The parents raised their eyebrows, but the kids beamed. My girls scored tons of goals this way, which eventually gave them the confidence to score more conventional goals.

There are a couple of lessons here. First, if something is working for you, keep doing it. Don't switch to doing what you think is expected—it might not be better. Second, I am a person who tunes in to the smiles, not the raised eyebrows. Whatever works, works, even if it seems a little strange to other people.

Turns out you can go pretty far as a girls' soccer coach if you pay attention to the cartwheels and the crying. Coaching wisdom is really wisdom for living every day: seeing the goal ahead and identifying the simplest strategies to get there.

My cross-country star with the panic attacks? He comes back in two weeks, smiling. He's running again and making friends with other runners. He's in a routine that feels right for him. His panic attacks have resolved and he's adjusting to college. I don't need to see him again. "Oh, Doctor," he says on the way out, "my mom says thanks; she thought you were going to put me on medication."

The students almost never thank me, but the moms sometimes do. It's one of my favorite parts of my job.

■ ■ ■

About that job. I am a senior staff psychiatrist in the counseling center at Boston University. The views expressed throughout *How to Thrive at College* are my own and do not represent the official position of Boston University.

My colleagues and I at the BU counseling center exist for students in crisis. There are around thirty of us serving a population of approximately 30,000 students. Together, we see about 150 students a day. That's 150 conversations a day with young adults, eighteen to twenty-five years old, approximately 180 days a year. (Summers are slower, unless there's a pandemic going on, and if you are a careful reader, you've already noticed that I have the summers off. But I'm getting ahead of myself.) But who's counting? I love this job. My editor made me share those stats.

Most of the young people who visit our office are experiencing symptoms that will resolve in a matter of days or weeks. They don't know that, but we do.

We have seen everything.

Lemme Go!

Call them back! Want your parents to stop texting, calling, pestering, and otherwise interrupting your day? Reply to them! Seriously! Parents usually just want to know that you're okay, and when they can expect to hear from you. So send a quick reply letting them know when a good time would be to catch up and follow through by calling them at the agreed time. Then they will leave you alone. *Mostly.*

CHAPTER TWO

If It's Not Working, Change It Up.

The patient in my office is anxious. She worries about everything—you name it: grades, the future, getting sick, crowds, being alone. It's affecting her body. She has stomach problems and heart palpitations; she can't sleep. She's honestly miserable, and she's in my office to talk about medication.

This is Generalized Anxiety Disorder. I spend a lot of time talking about anxiety, because it presents an interesting problem. Many of the things I deal with are clearly illnesses. Most people would agree that a psychotic person is clearly ill; same goes for someone who is too depressed to get out of bed.

Anxiety is more of a continuum, and there's a sweet spot. Everybody has some, and, frankly, you need it to function. It does good things like make you pay your bills on time, work on your term paper before the deadline, or call your mom back. Having some anxiety makes you function better. But having too much can cause real problems—like upset stomachs, insomnia, poor concentration, or locking yourself in the bathroom because you're afraid to go out. When to call it a disorder is a bit of a judgment call, but to paraphrase the old saying: *it's anyone more anxious than I am.*

So we have anxiety disorders, and this is Generalized Anxiety Disorder.

Except it's not. Because this is Caffeine Dependence. It's indistinguishable from Generalized Anxiety Disorder unless you take the time to really find out how much someone is sleeping and how much caffeine they are using.

Caffeine, sleep deprivation, and anxiety exist in a vicious cycle, each making the other worse. Sleep deprivation alone can cause a stress response, which makes you a little anxious, even though you're tired. The caffeine helps with the fatigue, but also makes your anxiety worse, and makes it more likely that you won't sleep well the next night. So, this cycle continues, leading to more and more caffeine use and less and less sleep until you are in my office with what you think is an anxiety disorder. Which is a reasonable thing to think, because Caffeine Dependence is indistinguishable from an anxiety disorder, and you are not a psychiatrist.

So she doesn't need medication for anxiety, because all she needs to do is cut back on caffeine, and her problematic anxiety will resolve. So we'll just talk about normal sleep requirements and the impact of caffeine use, and she'll make a few changes in her life and live happily ever after.

Except she won't. She wants an SSRI. You've probably heard about selective serotonin reuptake inhibitors because they're constantly in the newspaper. Depending on the day, SSRIs are either the *cause of* or the *solution to* all the world's problems. (It's hard to keep up, even for me.) She wants medication because cutting back on caffeine would also cause her to need to sleep more, which would cause her to miss something important, like a sorority meeting or something. So she doesn't like my plan.

You wouldn't believe how often this happens. In all the times I've encountered this situation, many take my advice, and adopt a lifestyle that allows them to sleep more. Some can't; some students are stretched so thin financially that they have to work more hours than is reasonable just to make ends meet. For these students, I'm happy to prescribe.

But too many want the SSRI for convenience, as a short-cut. And I'm hard pressed to prescribe it in those instances. They don't want to cut back—quit a club, reduce lab hours, take a smaller part in a play. Instead of giving them a prescription, I tell them what I think: For most people, being happy isn't too complicated if you listen to your body and make small adjustments when you're not doing well. But it's also your life, so if you're not interested in my opinion then I'm going to save my energy for someone who is. But you're welcome to come back for my guidance if you change your mind.

■ ■ ■

The next student is a philosophy major. Well, that's what her profile on the computer in front of me says, so she must be. She's smart and intellectual and wants to go to grad school to study philosophy, but there's just one thing she needs my help with: She's too depressed to go to class so she needs medicine. And this sounds serious, so I am happy to discuss it, because medicine is sometimes helpful.

I believe in medicine, but I also believe in thoroughness. So I ask about other things, which is pretty much what psychiatrists do all day. And not just stereotypical questions like, "how do you feel?" because that is a rather dispiriting question to ask when you spend most of your day talking to people who are depressed or anxious.

I ask her questions about her life, because that's more interesting and I'm the doctor in this scenario. Questions like, "what do you do during the time that you're not sitting around being too depressed to go to philosophy class?"

And the answer is . . . most days she gets up at four in the morning to go to her job making bread at a local bakery, which she loves. You may not know much about college, but I can tell you with a high degree of certainty that not many students wake up at four in the morning to do just about anything. And they certainly don't do it happily! She talks about bread making like she's talking about poetry, but she talks about philosophy like she's talking about . . . well, philosophy.

So now I'm thinking that maybe it's not that she's too depressed to go to philosophy class, but more likely that philosophy is too depressing for her. Because philosophy is not for everyone. I'm starting to think that her primary problem is that the computer in front of me says she's a philosophy major, when she's actually a bread-making major.

But at a place like BU, you're not supposed to dream of making bread because that's manual labor and not using your brain, and using your brain is the route to a fulfilling life.

Well, other people think that, but I really like bread, especially when it's made by hand with love or placebo. And I also think there are eight billion other people who also need to eat every day, and perhaps helping to feed them could be . . . fulfilling?

I reply to her that sometimes depression is the body's way of communicating that something is wrong. And I suggest that instead of taking the medicine . . . maybe she should take the message.

■ ■ ■

Now there's another kid in my office with panic attacks.

I ask what's new and find out he began using marijuana with his friends every day when he came back to campus a few weeks ago and developed panic attacks soon after. He informs me there's no correlation. He thinks it's a coincidence and that he probably needs an SSRI. Because that's what the newspaper, which in his case is probably social media, says you need for panic attacks.

The students I meet are invariably smart and spend a lot of time thinking. But as in the case of my philosophy major, thinking can be problematic when it is overconfident and reinforces false logic.

This has made me very skeptical about thinking, in general.

On the face of it, there's no real way of knowing if someone's thinking is accurate or not, but in my case, I have an advantage. Because if you are in my office, you are probably unhappy, and it might be because of your thinking.

And in this student's case, he thinks his marijuana is not problematic.

But I think it is. I am older and more experienced and am not on a mind-altering substance. I also know what society has been telling him.

He believes what his thoughts are saying and not what his body is saying.

But the truth is marijuana *is* a problem for *him*.

So I'm trying to explain to him that he has to stop. But there is no persuading someone who believes he is right and has an addictive substance on board. All this talking about thinking has us quite stuck. It's also exhausting, and I have to save some energy for carpool! So I switch tactics. I offer him a bet. I tell him I think he is addicted to marijuana and that he probably can't go two weeks without using it.

He takes the bet.

When he comes back in two weeks, he's stopped smoking pot and he's laughing and talking about how his panic attacks stopped and how this is a huge relief. And he adds, "and you wouldn't believe how much better my asthma is."

Actually, I would.

▪ ▪ ▪

When someone is making a decision, they are often encouraged to "think about it." But I'm not convinced that thinking is always the best way to make decisions. In this case, our student had to stop thinking about whether marijuana was harming him and just try taking a break. There was no perfect clinical trial to guide his decision; he had to conduct an imperfect clinical trial on himself. He felt great after his clinical trial because his panic attacks stopped. This information might not be generalizable to other people, but it was critical information for him.

When our family decided to compost we argued about whether it would work well or be worth it; and the argument wasn't getting anywhere. Everyone was just getting locked into their position. So we decided to conduct our own clinical trial and just . . . try it.

Weirdly, composting made our lives better. The trash smelled better, and the dogs weren't getting into it as much. And did you know you can compost pizza boxes? I didn't either! This is life-changing information for a working mom. You see, kids more or less only eat pizza, but the boxes present a huge dilemma. Do you put them in the trash, and feel guilty about it, or do you sneak them into the recycling, which is generally not allowed, and feel guilty about *that*? Being a working mom comes with lots of guilt even before the pizza boxes, so composting is a revelation! And we are now a family that happily composts. Our imperfect clinical trial was much more productive than thinking and discussing and arguing, which honestly could have gone on forever.

Same holds if you're concerned about cellphones, or exercise, or fill-in-the-blank. If you're concerned about the mental health implications, just conduct an imperfect clinical trial on yourself. Imperfect research is not helpful for drawing conclusions about what is best for everyone, but it is perfect for you. Just go two weeks without using your phone or without pot or with running and see if your life is better. If it is, great. And if it's not, you haven't lost much.

Sometimes you have to just try something first and see if it's a good idea later. And I think a lot of Cognitive Behavioral Therapists might agree with me. Because they are also pretty skeptical of thinking (much more coming on CBT!).

Need help now?

Chores or attitude—pick one. If your teenager is taking out the trash when you asked them to, don't call them out on the eyeroll. They will take out the trash either on their own time or grumpily. A teenager happily taking out the trash at the exact moment you want them to is not a thing.

CHAPTER THREE

Some Truths, Fictions, Placebos, and Nocebos.

The girl in my office has been having intense mood swings for weeks. Crying spells, irritability, you name it. But not just that. She's also kind of bloated and has gained some weight. So I take a history. All these symptoms are new. She's never felt like this before. The general ick feeling started three months ago, and now she's pretty sure she's going crazy, which is what people who bother to come see me are often thinking. So I ask about other things that happened three months ago. And I learn that she started taking a birth control pill with a name with a rather high Scrabble score.

So I tell her the pill can do this to you, especially certain formulations with high Scrabble scores, and she should stop taking it, but not until three weeks later when she finishes this pack. And she does this and comes back two months later and tells me she's fine, back to herself.

A different girl has an overlapping story. She's miserable for a week every month, sometimes even suicidal, and it doesn't seem fair, or maybe even survivable, and she doesn't know what to do. So I tell her about the mood benefits of birth control and how it's not just for not getting pregnant, and it doesn't mean she has to have sex. And I send her to primary care.

She comes back two months later, and she's doing great. She's back to her old self, except better than that because her old self was suicidal about a quarter of the time.

So I ask her what pill she's taking, and she gives me a name with a rather high Scrabble score. I tell her that's great, because it's one of the best.

Sometimes my job is confusing, because X and the opposite of X can be true at the same time, and high school math didn't prepare me for that. But in this case, I guess I should be saying XX, because I'm a doctor after all.

So I told the first girl it's the worst one and the second girl it's the best one, because both are true and neither is true because the truth is there is no best one. There's only the one that is best for you.

But in the case of the second girl, I also wanted to give her some hope, which is essentially what we call placebo. You might be surprised to hear that placebo is science, and the way I know it's science is because placebo is how all the medications psychiatrists use work. We trick the brain into thinking something is better, and then . . . it's better. When your mom kisses your knee and says you'll get better and then you're better: That's placebo, and that's science.

So I give her some placebo, because being female is actually quite hard, but I'm constantly mixing up placebo and love, so it's possible I gave her some of that as well.

At least it doesn't have any side effects.

But that was then and this is now, and the pill with the rather high Scrabble score has been superseded by newer versions with even higher Scrabble scores. Because it was the worst birth control pill, or because it was the best? Because female physiology has completely changed in the last ten years? Because the pill has important side effects that the pharmaceutical industry is trying to improve upon? No, none of those things, though the latter is foreplay, I mean foreshadowing.

This particular pill went off patent and therefore became unprofitable. This happened around the same time I finally got used to dealing with the mysterious reactions people frequently had to it. Oh sure, the chemical compound exists and is probably available if you can get close enough to the correct pronunciation for your doctor to prescribe it. But there are so many names of chemical compounds, and they're so similar that it's really hard to keep track, so it's much easier to stick with a form of the pill that has a catchy brand name. Get it? It's almost like they planned it that way—making the generic names deliberately long and confusing and the brand names deliberately hip and catchy so the consumer, I mean patient, automatically keeps reaching for the new one. Actually, they did plan it that way. It's why pharmaceutical companies have such large marketing departments.

So, every year, numerous "new" medications appear on the market, some genuine improvements on what was previously available and some not, but all with catchy names and massive marketing budgets, and it's up to health care providers to sort through it. And we mostly do—it's our job, and we have quite a bit of training to guide us.

But there has been a movement to make the birth control pill available over the counter; that is, available to be purchased without a prescription. It is available in some places. This is promoted in the name of increasing freedom and choice for women, and people are enthusiastically discussing the idea in the media. However, whenever you subtract health care providers from the equation, you remove an opportunity for a patient to get unbiased information. That is to say it creates a situation that guarantees patients will primarily be getting their information from marketing departments, as opposed to health care providers. There might be a few problems with that—just saying.

▪ ▪ ▪

A student files in. He's depressed, but only a little. He's the kind of person that every newspaper says shouldn't take an SSRI, and in this case the newspapers are right. Because in this case he doesn't leave his room much or really ever go outside, and getting out would be really good for him.

But he's in my office and he wants an SSRI.

One rule you have to know about my job is that if the patient wants a medication, they probably don't need one, and if they actually need a medication they probably don't want to take one. So that is something you need to keep in mind, but it should be easy to remember because it doesn't make sense, and nothing about humans makes sense.

So he's asking for an SSRI, and I'm telling him to exercise more, but he's not interested in that because it's hard, and also because he's not sporty.

So I go into a digression about how youth sports have really lost their way, and some kids do too much and most kids do none, when really everyone should do some. And I probably drone on and on about how the adults have long since sucked the joy out of youth sports, and they're currently working their way through college sports. And I'm pretty sure I sound wise and sophisticated, but he's starting to look bored, so I better take this in a different direction.

It's not just that he's not sporty, it's that he doesn't have time. Because he's an English major. And I am extremely sensitive to the time constraints facing English majors, because some things never change. I'm not going to make any progress arguing about how much time he has—English majors definitely have no free time.

But he's also an intellectual from a certain kind of city, so in a moment of frustration I might have (definitely) said, "I've heard that Barack Obama exercises for an hour a day; you can too." I hope I said it nicely.

And he perked right up, and the next time I saw him he was exercising regularly. Outside. Which is what I was trying to get him to do when we were at a crossroads about the SSRI.

Well, I was so impressed at the success of this intervention that I started to do it with other students.

Taking into consideration the number of times a week that I talk about exercise and multiply that by my years at BU and you get . . . I have probably spoken that sentence over a thousand times. Without permission. And without even knowing if it were true.

President Obama, if you're reading, I just sort of figured you wouldn't mind. Due to your inspiration, there might be a generation of young people who aren't sporty but now exercise regularly to keep themselves happy. But there also might not be, because exercise is hard, and definitely a lot harder than taking an SSRI. And if you're not exercising an hour a day then you better start, because you have a reputation to keep up.

▪ ▪ ▪

I'm running a little late (again), so I quickly check the name of my next patient, whom I haven't met before, and run to the waiting room to get her. Only I get so distracted by an extremely beautiful woman who is sitting out there that I forget my patient's name and have to run back to my office.

When I come back to the waiting room and call the name . . . the beautiful woman gets up. This woman is actually one of the most beautiful people I have ever seen in person, and quite possibly even a little more beautiful than my husband says I am. But let's be honest, his glasses are getting a bit thick.

We sit down in my office, and I start by asking why she came to BU, which is the way I usually start. Turns out she used to be a model, but she changed her mind and decided to go to college, because modeling was killing her. Literally. Not the kind of killing that comedians do, or the kind of killing where you have a little bit of extra time at the airport, so you go look at fashion magazines. No, the kind where a malnourished and dehydrated person has to stand under hot lights for hours on end without moving or drinking water and then passes out and hits her head and gets rushed to the hospital. That's the kind of killing I'm talking about.

I guess to understand why she was so malnourished and dehydrated, you have to understand a little bit about modeling. The way it works is they take a small number of people who are extremely attractive and tell them to get just a little bit more attractive. It's important that they get a little bit more attractive because one of a model's most important jobs is to make the rest of the women feel bad about themselves. And they could do this ever so slightly better if they make themselves more attractive. And the way to do that is mostly by doing things that are quite bad for you. Like not eating.

So being around all those people in the industry who were constantly telling her she needed to be a little more . . . or a little less . . . made her believe she was ugly. When she was not ugly at all. Actually, she looked quite a bit like Gwyneth Paltrow.

I have a beef with Gwyneth Paltrow. That is, I have a beef with her currently, not back when I was sitting in my office listening to the story of a perfectly healthy woman who almost died from a head injury she incurred in the name of fashion.

My beef with Gwyneth Paltrow is not about the ski incident. Okay, it's a *little* bit about that. I think she can be criticized for skiing at Deer Valley. Everyone knows that no one at Deer Valley knows how to ski! Obviously not, because you don't go there to ski. You mostly go there to drink hot chocolate and sit in hot tubs and worry about whether everyone else there is richer or a better skier. Well, you don't have to worry about the latter, because I can tell you they're not. No serious skier would ever be caught dead at Deer Valley.

You've probably guessed that I'm not exactly an early adopter, and that also applies to skiing. I am honestly somewhat suspicious of any ski area that has anything more modern than a rope tow. Not just because it's a sign of selling out. Because rope tows were *hard*. And things that are hard often teach you something. In the case of rope tows, what they teach you is . . . how to ski.

Just in case you were born after 1980 or don't ski, what a rope tow does is tow you up the mountain on your skis, so you can ski down with just gravity. You see rope tows are, well, were so hard, that it was nearly impossible to learn how to use them. You had to practice a lot. So, by the time you could get to the top of the mountain on a rope tow, you could probably safely ski down. Which is good, because gravity doesn't care if you know how to ski. It sort of just does its thing, which is physics, and the slope is slippery, which in this case is the point. Learning to ski on a rope tow reminds me of Cognitive Behavioral Therapy; you have to do something hard to make things easy.

Well, this was honestly a good idea because skiing, like many things that are fun, can also have dangerous side effects. Like people crashing into each other. No one at Deer Valley has ever heard of primitive things like rope tows, so they definitely can't ski safely down a mountain. Which is why serious skiers go somewhere else.

There's also the issue of the bathrooms with gold-plated toilets and orchids on the shelves, so there's nowhere to put your gloves.

But my beef with Gwyneth Paltrow isn't about skiing at Deer Valley; it's about "wellness." It seems to me that her brand embodies a kind of "wellness for sale" culture—which, if you ask me, often leaves women feeling worse rather than better, while taking quite a bit of their money.

As far as I can tell, to get a woman to spend several hundred dollars on something she doesn't need, you first have to make her think that there's something wrong with her. Like maybe there's something wrong with her private body parts. And women don't always know if there's something wrong with private body parts because no one ever talks about it. So they might just listen to someone famous.

To get the word out, you have to use advertising, and that means using really beautiful women like the one in my office because the whole system works a little better if the women also have to compare themselves to the beautiful woman in the ad. Who has sacrificed so much to make herself beautiful that she ended up in the hospital.

So I have beef with Gwyneth Paltrow. I don't think wellness can be sold in a jar—though celebrity wellness brands sometimes make it look that way. In my admittedly idiosyncratic view, the whole industry seems built on making women feel bad enough to buy the cure. She should know all too well that women often get the raw end of things. So, when they make a movie about my life, I won't be played by Gwyneth Paltrow! (Even though some people think she's almost as beautiful.)

Back to the student in my office. While she was in the hospital, her parents came and encouraged her to go to college instead of modeling. Because luckily, she had parents like that. Well, considering the psychological aftermath I am dealing with here I sort of wish they had intervened a little earlier, because you may recall that I was already running behind schedule. But at least they did something, before it was too late, to get her off her slippery slope.

When I was driving carpool recently, my daughter and her friends were all talking about a girl they know who is a model and was recently in a famous magazine, the kind you might flip through killing time in the airport.

They're all talking and laughing to each other. I'm pretending not to listen but hoping I'll find an opportunity to say something.

Here I should say something about carpool. Everyone is always talking about how important family dinner is, because that's when families talk about things. Except it's not. At the dinner table, people mostly argue about whose turn it is to walk the dog and do the dishes, as well as whether anyone needs a ride tomorrow or more money. If you bring up anything else, even if it's important to talk about, everyone acts uninterested and pretends to have homework. No, if you want to talk about something important with kids you have to do it during carpool, which is when things come up naturally. Not naturally in the sense of natural skin products, which are mostly advertising and not natural at all, but natural in the sense of something that just happens.

So I'm looking for a subtle way to join the conversation about modeling, because by now it's making me uncomfortable. Happily, I don't have to work very hard, because they ask me.

"Don't you think it's cool that this girl we all know is in a famous magazine?"

And I swallow my pride, privately acknowledge I'm not cool, and answer.

"No. I don't think it's cool. I think it's adults making money off a child's body and that crosses a line for me. And maybe the family is using the money for college savings because college is expensive. But even so, there are other adults making money, like agents and magazines, and I don't think there's anything cool about it at all."

This is quite possibly the least cool thing I have ever said, but it happens to be what I think.

Lemme Go!

Because they love you, that's why. This is the answer to all of your questions about your parents' weird and annoying behavior. Why do they pester/nag/micromanage/overreact/fill-in-the-blank so much? Love.

This isn't love in the sense that a six-year-old loves the color blue or an eleven-year-old loves Cheez-Its or a fourteen-year-old loves Taylor Swift. This is entirely different. Have you ever watched a nature documentary? Have you ever seen a gazelle throw herself between her fawn and a crocodile? Trying to distract or counterattack? *The sad futility.*

This is the software package that evolution has equipped your parents with, to handle such catastrophes as your returning home fifteen minutes past curfew, or your soccer coach not giving you enough playing time. Yes, they overreact and can be quite difficult to reason with. *But did you see the size of that crocodile?*

CHAPTER FOUR

WWYDFYD? (What Would You Do for Your Dog?)

The next student in my office wants to do better in school. Already. In September. This is a pretty common reason for students to come see me. He wants to do better in school and plans to see if I am a vending machine for Adderall. He had read about Adderall in the newspaper and is pretty sure he needs it.

You see, he's currently studying for ten hours a day, and thinks an Adderall prescription would allow him to study for twelve hours a day, which would obviously make him do better in school.

Okay, no human can do high-level work for twelve hours a day on an ongoing basis and college students are, last I checked, human. It's a recipe for exhaustion and burnout, not to mention being unhappy, which people in my office generally are. When kids dream of college, they don't dream of spending time in the mental health clinic, so no one wants to meet me. When they do, it's frequently because, to a surprising degree, college students don't know how to take care of themselves.

So early on, I developed a thought experiment to help young people understand the importance of self-care. I ask if they had a family dog while they were growing up. When the answer is "yes," I ask what the dog needs to stay happy and healthy. They usually come up with food and water quickly. Then they come up with exercise—everyone kind of knows that their dog gets a little crazy without exercise. It generally takes a little bit of coaching to get students to come up with sleep, even though dogs sleep most of the time. A dog without sleep is like a toddler without sleep, and no one wants to be around a sleep-deprived toddler.

By this point, they think the thought experiment is over, and that they have passed the test. But I'm just getting started. Because there is one thing the family dog needs more than any of the things we have covered so far. Love. (You can call it placebo if you're more comfortable with that.) You see, without high doses of love or placebo, your family dog isn't your dog at all—it's just an animal living in your house. Everyone knows a family dog isn't just an animal, although most people have trouble describing how or why. The how or why is *empathic attunement*—the thing that makes your dog your dog, and everyone else's dog . . . annoying. It's the difference between a close friend and someone you've just met. It's also the difference between loving your toddler and thinking other people shouldn't be allowed to bring toddlers on the plane. Anyway, dogs are particularly awesome at empathic attunement, which is one of the reasons they are so great for teenagers.

The dog metaphor is great for explaining self-care, but it also provides a decent framework for parenting. Moreover, children and puppies recognize love in about the same way. That is to say, a puppy doesn't recognize it as love if you say "I love you," and proceed to spend all your time making money so you can pay for an expensive education and then fuss that the grades he is getting are not worth the tuition you are paying. If your puppy wouldn't recognize it as love, chances are your child doesn't. (For the purposes of this passage, "child" is defined as anyone under the age of twenty-five whom you have been raising.) I have met young people with very expensive educations who have had seriously neglectful childhoods. Lots of them. What children and puppies recognize as love is undivided attention, playful interaction, your delighted expression, and lots of laughing and goofing around, all with safe boundaries and appropriate limits.

Anyway, about half the time I give my dog spiel, the student sitting before me has a family dog, and really gets the metaphor. But this student doesn't have a dog, so I need to think of something else. And the first thing that comes to mind is . . . Yo-Yo Ma. Yes, during my years at BU, I've spent a surprising amount of time talking about Yo-Yo Ma. It's surprising because I'm not a musician and don't know much about music. But I'm a big fan of

Bach's *Cello Suites*, as they are great for putting children to sleep, specifically my children, which meant I could then sleep. So I asked the student if he had heard of Yo-Yo Ma, and luckily, he had. Then the conversation went something like this:

"How many hours a day do you think Yo-Yo Ma practices?"

"Twelve hours."

Twelve hours?! That is commonly the first guess. Where on earth do they learn this stuff? (You're going to find out, but we haven't gotten there yet.) Can you imagine doing anything for twelve hours per day, let alone doing that thing well, let alone being a virtuoso?

After I scrape the shock off my face, I start gently challenging this answer. What about fatigue? What about making mistakes? After a certain point, he'd be tired, and inevitably make mistakes, so he'd be rehearsing the mistakes, making himself worse, not better. Never mind how demanding it would be physically. How much does a cello weigh? Have you ever met anyone who works out for twelve hours a day? And what about the passion in his music? Could he maintain that for twelve hours a day? Of course not! He's Yo-Yo Ma, not an AI. Humans have limits and need all the things that family dogs need.

With this line of thinking, I can usually work students down to about six to eight hours per day. My goal is honestly four to six, and I think it might be less than that. But I tell them I generally think most humans have about six to eight good hours in them per day, and anything more is just diminishing returns, or maybe making things worse. And this is generally how learning works. You learn best by doing something frequently, not by doing it to the point of exhaustion. For example, I have learned the street addresses of every pharmacy in the greater Boston area. It's true! I send in prescriptions electronically. For each one, you need to confirm the pharmacy's street address. Anyway, the students usually can't remember where they live, so I have to tell them which pharmacy is closest to their apartment . . . so they can find their way home. Do this a few times a day over several years and before you know it . . . you know the street address of every pharmacy within a ten-mile radius of your office with no effort at all. That's how learning works!

So I tell the student that I think he needs to be studying less, not more, and that I think he will do better in school if he does, not to mention have more fun and be happier, which not coincidentally, is associated with better learning. And I may or may not have remembered to refer him to the appropriate office to tune his study skills so he could work more efficiently, which is different from working more.

As you can imagine, throughout the years I was using Yo-Yo Ma as a model, a nagging feeling was growing in me. What if Yo-Yo Ma really was an AI and rehearsed for twelve hours a day? Have I been misleading young people and encouraging better work-life balance, depriving them of a dramatic midlife crisis when they turn fifty? So, one day, when I saw an interview with Yo-Yo Ma in the *New York Times*, I immediately read it. It was pretty long, and I was biting my nails and crossing my fingers and holding my breath and hoping against hope that the interviewer would ask: How much do you practice every day?

He did. He asked, and the answer . . . well it made my whole day—decade, in fact, since I'm obviously still talking about it. He gave a long-winded answer with all the variables that you would expect, such as what performances were coming up or how he was feeling, but basically what I remember is that he said . . . sometimes as little as fifteen minutes a day.

Need help now?

Never have a conversation with a hungry teenager. Just don't. Let them eat first.

■ ■ ■

The next student is already worrying about going home. Come again? It's only September! He clarifies that he has to travel home for a wedding in a couple of weeks, and he is afraid of flying. Well, he technically doesn't *need* to fly, but the alternative is driving forty-eight hours, attending the wedding, and driving forty-eight hours back. This would only be a little better for the environment than flying, so he has a plane ticket.

This student has a panic attack every time he gets on a plane. Not the have-a-few-too-many glasses of wine during the flight kind that you see all the time. This is the true reason flight attendants are so liberal with alcohol. It's not because it makes the airlines money; it's because some of these people would otherwise be having panic attacks. (I don't know why they have the rule that you can't bring your own alcohol on the plane—maybe that's to make the airlines money. I don't make up the rules. But I *should*.)

No, this is the kind of panic attack that makes them ground the airplane at the nearest airport because they think you are having a medical emergency. Well, it is a medical emergency, but not the kind they think.

So this student has to get on a plane in two weeks, and he is already having anticipatory insomnia. Every night, he is dreading this flight when he should be sleeping.

Luckily, there is effective treatment for phobias: Exposure Therapy, which is a form of Cognitive Behavioral Therapy. Turns out, you can inoculate yourself against any phobia by exposing yourself to the thing you are afraid of. I usually explain this by talking about arachnophobia, which everyone familiar with movies from the nineties will immediately recognize as fear of spiders.

The basic idea is that you gradually expose an individual to increasingly anxiety-provoking stimuli. After the patient habituates to a low-level exposure, they are ready to advance. For example, you might start with just thinking about spiders or maybe reading *Charlotte's Web*. Then you graduate to talking about spiders. Over a period of weeks, you build up to looking at pictures of spiders, and then maybe looking at a spider in a box at a distance, and then maybe up close, and then maybe opening the box, and then maybe holding the spider in your hand. And then jumping into a swimming pool full of spiders, I think. I don't know, I'm not really a CBT therapist.

Anyway, you can do this with flying. Logan airport had a program for a while, but anyone with a little CBT training can do it. The basic idea is, you start with sitting in a classroom at the airport and talking about planes, and later you step on a plane with your instructor, and eventually you get on a plane with your instructor and fly somewhere.

So I'm explaining this to the student, and he's looking at me like there isn't time before the wedding. But I'm mostly telling him all this to point out the absurd degree to which our culture values facing and overcoming your fears, even if your fear is hurtling through the atmosphere in a small metal tube. We haven't evolved to fly, and some humans are, quite reasonably, afraid of it.

I'm not recommending Exposure Therapy. I'm prescribing medication to prevent panic attacks on travel days.

"It's not worth it," I say; "you only fly a few times a year."

Another student is afraid of dogs. Can't be near them. Crosses the street if she sees one. If she touches one, she has a panic attack that derails the rest of her day. She can't say why—is she afraid of being bitten, or germs, or an allergic reaction, or getting dog hair on her sweater?

She doesn't know. The fact is, when she sees or even really thinks about a dog, it throws her into a stress response, and all bets are off. She doesn't remember how or when it started, and it's long since become a conditioned response.

She moved off campus for the current academic year and didn't realize how many dogs lived in her new neighborhood. Walking to class is becoming a major problem. She can walk by a dog park where there will definitely be dogs or go several blocks out of the way. But she still might see a dog if she goes the long way, and she might be late for class.

This is why she has come to see me. Her plan is to take medication for a couple of years so she can live near the dog park without having panic attacks every day, and then after graduation she's going to move to a place with fewer dogs.

"Sorry," I say, "you're going to have to learn to live with them."

There's no such thing as a place without dogs, and there never will be. How do I know? Do I know that the emotional support animal craze is coming, and everyone will have to sit next to a dog every time they hurtle through the atmosphere in a small metal tube? Do I know that a pandemic is coming, and the local dog population is going to grow so much that I can no longer get an appointment with my veterinarian?

No. I know that humans have been living with dogs since before we were modern humans. Before we had farming, or horses, or math, or maybe even language, we had dogs. I know that anthropologists have recently found the ancient remains of a small child, and the child was buried with a dog.

So this stuff about humans and dogs runs deep, and you can't avoid it.

This is a job for Exposure Therapy.

October—Mid-Terms and Parents' Weekend

CHAPTER FIVE
Mid-Terms

Coaching girls' soccer forced me to develop skills braiding hair. I discovered early on that they played better if they could see. When their hair was in their eyes, they frequently seemed shocked when the ball suddenly appeared in their field of vision. When their hair was up, they mostly seemed to know what was going on. Depending on the kid, there were many other variables that affected their attention and response time, but this was a variable within my control. So I braided a lot of hair.

Before a game in early October, I'm on my third or fourth pair of braids, and something isn't right. Something is moving in her hair. Lots of things. I had an assistant coach at the time who was super useful, because he knew the rules of soccer. That sure came in handy! Also, he was a pediatrician. A side effect of being a pediatrician is that he was terrible with names because he had so many kids to keep track of. (He was also a tiny bit absent-minded and once left a girl at practice, which had a happy ending because it resulted in a sleepover at my house.) But *anyhoo*, on this particular day, a pediatrician was just what I needed.

I quietly ask him to come take a look. He takes a quick look, and nods without changing his expression. He calls the relevant mom, and I finish braiding. Well, I couldn't stop, could I? We still had a game in five minutes, and she still had a hair situation! Maybe the braids will hold the lice in. Shrug.

The pediatrician and I look at each other and contemplate what to do. There are no cartwheels or tears involved, so everything is fine as far as I'm concerned. He suggests that we try to limit the huddling. But this is girls' soccer, so we obviously fail. I guess I'll just email the team parents later. Shrug.

Some people think the academic year should be longer, but schools hold on to the summer vacation model because it gives the lice population time to die back. Seriously! Lice have a life cycle, and they can't survive all that time without kids! So September is essentially lice-free. But summer camp and siblings allow a small number to survive the summer and repopulate the schools. By October, they're back in full swing.

Back at BU, things are also in full swing. Bigger kids are starting to take mid-terms, and I'm starting to hear about it. One hectic morning I finish with a patient and open my door to find Mitzi standing there with a look on her face. She whispers that someone is here without an appointment, which is tricky on a busy day. But the situation is that the girl has an exam in twenty minutes and she wants to ask me if she has schizophrenia.

I know this girl well, because she is my patient. She has obsessive compulsive disorder, which is a problem of thinking and doing. Like thinking about contamination and then quickly washing your hands. But many people with OCD no longer have the doing; they just have thinking and unthinking.

A related aside, at age two when my son was learning about rules and safety, he would walk around our apartment and get very close to each electrical socket and announce, "Don't touch. Good boy. Don't touch. Good boy. Don't touch. Good boy." He grew out of it, because that's what children do. Consequently, I'm convinced that there is a pretty good reason that OCD is common in humans, having something to do with safety. But if you are an adult, you might not grow out of it, and it can become problematic.

And in this girl's case, it is. She has a frequent intrusive thought that she might have schizophrenia. She doesn't, but it's quite a reasonable thought, because her brother does. So she has this intrusive thought that she might have schizophrenia, which we have discussed quite a bit. She doesn't have it, but the thought persists.

Running to my office before an exam is *reassurance-seeking*. Which for her, is a little like handwashing. Meaning it's okay once in a while, but not too much. The intervention that would help her is a kind of Cognitive Behavioral Therapy called Exposure and Response Prevention (ERP), which is the gold standard for treating OCD.

The basic idea of ERP is that when you have the thought you don't do the action; you just sit with the thought until it goes away, even though it's uncomfortable. And then you see that you're okay without the action and learn that the thought is just thinking and thinking is . . . highly overrated sometimes.

If you learn to just sit with it, the thinking will eventually get better. For her the thinking is wondering if she has schizophrenia and the action is running to my office for reassurance. And if you are an ERP therapist you know that if someone comes to your office seeking reassurance you should . . . definitely not reassure them. But ERP outcomes are based on six-month clinical trials, and she's not in a clinical trial. She's in college. And she has an exam in twenty minutes.

Luckily for this student, I am Board Certified in psychiatry and have learned that there are alternative ways of looking at just about everything . . . like complicated psychoanalytic theories with elaborate and serious-sounding names . . . written by people who other people listen to . . . backed by numerous articles all denying the obvious, which is that psychoanalytic theory was mostly made up.

Never mind all that. One thing all these erudite theories all agree on is that patients should not be seen without an appointment. There are very elaborate rationalizations for this—involving boundaries and lots of other three-syllable words. But they boil down to . . . well, this is really inconvenient for the therapist, who can't bill in this situation.

So, I should probably ignore this drop-in student altogether.

Instead, I say to Mitzi, "Sure, send her in." And I give the student a few seconds of my ears and remind her that we have already discussed this, and she doesn't have schizophrenia and say, "Good luck on your test."

▪ ▪ ▪

The next student is in a tizzy. Upset about an exam she just got back. She's telling me she's never going to pass this class, her life is a waste, she's going to be a total failure, and she absolutely shouldn't have gotten into BU.

I see a version of this all the time, and it can be tricky to decipher the reality of the situation. College is hard, and some kids aren't used to the workload. Occasionally, a kid actually is on the verge of failing out, and you definitely don't want to assume they're not. So I've learned to listen for a while and find shortcuts to uncover how much trouble the student is in. Are you on academic probation? Have you ever failed a class? Have you ever failed an exam?

If the answers are all "no," or if the student is dodging eye contact, or if I just have a hunch, the problem is most likely perfectionism. I meet a significant number of young people who have never gotten a grade below an A and totally fall apart at the thought of it.

To understand the degree of perfectionism, I sometimes want to know the actual grade. What's the level of failure that sent this individual running to my office? Is her scholarship in jeopardy, because her grade is near the cut-off? Or is it below the minimum required to remain in her major? Or is it an A–, a grade that could forever blemish a perfect 4.0?

So I just ask. She's totally freaking out, and I don't know her, so I'm not sure what I'm dealing with.

It's a 97.

CHAPTER SIX

They Want You to Come for Parents' Weekend . . . Unless They Don't . . . They Might Not Answer You Directly If You Ask Them . . . Good Luck!

Parents' Weekend is coming up, and there's a girl in my office crying about her father. Only she's mumbling "father" like he's Voldemort and she's not allowed to say his name. I must have looked confused, because then she says it louder, like "My Father," the way people do in church. So now I'm thinking he's not Voldemort but actually some kind of god, which I quickly learn is kind of right.

She stops crying enough to explain to me who her father is. Apparently, everyone except me already knows. And I must not have looked very interested, because instead of continuing to talk about her father . . . she talks about what's bothering her: Her father isn't coming for parents' weekend.

He has an emergency sporting event or contract negotiation or something. And this emergency is more important than his daughter. That's what he says with his actions, anyway. Or at least that's how she feels right now.

Her father isn't coming for parents' weekend, and all her friends' fathers are. And as you might be able to guess, a father whom everyone but me has heard of, because he runs a famous sports team . . . has probably done this before. Lots of times. Her whole life. So that's what she tells me about.

But what she doesn't tell me about are all the times when he did what he promised. And the reason for this is that crying is very good at making you remember. It makes you remember all the other times you've cried. And that's the basis of Cognitive Behavioral Therapy.

It's true. The basic idea is that crying makes you think about things that are sad, and things that are sad make you cry, so you just go on thinking and crying and crying and thinking until it's basically all you do. So emotional memory is quite effective—it makes you remember things very well. But there's one slight problem—emotional memory is self-reinforcing, and therefore not necessarily accurate.

Luckily you can also do the opposite, which is thinking less and crying less, which leads to less crying and less thinking, and that's Cognitive Behavioral Therapy. CBT is hard, which is how it works. It's like learning to ski on a rope tow.

But she's not interested in learning how CBT works yet. She's still all in on crying about her father, so I need to stay with her for the moment.

You see, she doesn't usually cry about her father. She doesn't feel entitled to, because she's lucky to have such a wonderful father. At least, that's what everyone tells her. But she is a little bit unsure. Anyone is allowed to cry in my office, which means you can cry there even if you don't otherwise feel entitled to. And I usually have tissues, unless I can't find them.

By this point, I'm feeling that her dad may be a bit of a jerk, and I may have said this aloud. I don't think sporting events and contract negotiations are more important than daughters, and I probably also said this. And she relaxes a little more and stops crying.

So we are able to have a conversation about fathers and daughters. This is something I know a lot about, because in addition to being a psychiatrist, I have a father, and I have a husband who is also a father. Everything you need to know about fathers and daughters is easy to summarize because there is already a stereotype: Fathers will do anything for their daughters. Especially if their daughter is crying. But to do any of the things that fathers do when their daughters cry, like flying across the country at the drop of a hat or committing assault against teenage boys or bankrupting themselves for Taylor Swift tickets, they need to know she's crying.

So I encourage her to call her father.

But I don't instruct her to tell him that I think he's a jerk, although that would be sort of fun. He won't care what I say, and besides, he's already gotten that feedback from a number of athletes and sports journalists, or so my husband says. But I also know that he will probably listen to her, and he definitely will if he knows she's been crying.

While we're talking, she comes to realize that while she loves her father, she doesn't love being seen as just his daughter.

So I encourage her to say this to him. And she does. She also tells him she doesn't like being treated like a meeting that can be rescheduled. Because that's how it feels to her. It makes her feel like sporting events and contract negotiations are more important than daughters. Even though she knows they're not. But knowing isn't always the same as feeling.

I'm not sure if he listened but she never came back, which in my world is usually a really good sign. But I think he did listen, because I know about fathers and daughters.

Or maybe she got rid of her cell phone and that's why she's fine. Because now, no one can call her and say that her father's not coming after all.

Need help now?

If they want to spend time with you, the answer is yes. This is a tricky one, because they're a little awkward about asking directly. For example, your teenager might ask you to drive them somewhere. Translation? They want to spend time with you. So do it. What if they ask you to drive them and some friends to an amusement park or a movie? You're taking them, and you're paying, even though your teenager is going to ignore you the whole time. Even if it's *A Minecraft Movie*. This is the teenager equivalent of their inner toddler sitting in your lap blowing raspberries in your face. Savor it!

Lemme Go!

Tell them if you want them to come for Parents' Weekend. And tell them if you don't. And please, tell them clearly, with enough lead time to make or cancel travel plans. There are a million good reasons for either preference, but it saves my office quite a few phone calls if *your* parents know *your* preference.

CHAPTER SEVEN

Your Approval: It's All They Want, Which Is a Little Confusing Because They Mostly Ignore You.

A colleague in another department has walked a student over to our office because she can't stop crying. I'm not exactly available, but my office is really close to the front door, so the student gets to see me.

It's true that she can't stop crying, so I let her cry for a while. That's easy, and I even have tissues in my office. Well, usually I do, but they always run out when someone is crying, and my office likes to keep me sharp by hiding the tissues in a different cabinet every week. Or maybe I just forget where they go.

So, I finally have tissues, and she's finally talking. Something terrible happened over the weekend. She drank more than she should have, and got separated from her friends, and had to take a taxi home by herself, and left her wallet in the taxi. So she can't stop crying.

Phew, a lost wallet. That's about the best-case scenario, considering where we started. I can totally handle this. Talk through the contents of the wallet, think through what needs to be deactivated or replaced, patch her up with some breathing exercises, and off she goes.

Nope, that's not where this goes. She's still halfway to a full-blown panic attack, so it's starting to feel like I am missing something. So that's what

I say. And she replies, "I'm afraid to tell my mom, because she's going to be mad at me."

I can't believe what I'm hearing. This girl was in a series of highly risky situations, came out relatively unscathed, and what she is afraid of is talking to her mom.

Is this mom a psychopath, or abusive? No, she's an ordinary mom. I know because we called her. I thought it would be a good idea for the student to call from my office, in case the conversation went badly. And her mom replied, "Are you okay?" and proceeded to problem-solve about the lost wallet. Because that's what an ordinary mom does.

So is this student hypersensitive, or paranoid? Also no. I have now seen a version of this so many times that I am convinced people in this age group, although they resemble adults, still look to their parents for approval like they did when they were in diapers. Parents loom large in their children's eyes, and it doesn't end when they go to college. Or maybe even ever.

It's easy to be fooled, though. They do things like write thesis papers and grow beards and roll their eyes at politicians, so it is very easy to think they've grown up. But if something very good or very bad happens to them, you will be the first person they think about. And they will be imagining your reaction.

I am not the only one who thinks like this. I had to go to a driver's ed parent training, where they teach you all kinds of useful things about helping your teenager learn to drive. Well, mostly they teach you about doing paperwork and standing in line at the DMV. But they also talk to you about teenagers and drunk driving. Serious people study this stuff.

When researchers interview teenagers who have survived a wreck and ask why they got into a car, what do you think they find? Did the teenager not realize the driver was drunk? Did they not know this was a bad idea? Were they too drunk to read the situation? Was their phone broken? All no.

The number one reason teenagers get in cars with drunk drivers instead of calling you, their parent, is that they are afraid you will be mad at them. Think about that for a moment.

All of this has had a significant effect on my parenting. When each of our children got phones, they immediately entered all their friends' numbers into their contacts, of course. With a little encouragement, they also entered the numbers for my husband and me. (Actually, we did that for them, but I'm sure they would have wanted us to.) Next, we discussed other adults they might want to program into their phones, so they would have someone to call in case of emergency. Someone who isn't their parents.

This took some doing, because it seemed a little strange to them. My older son was thirteen when we were going through this, and he asked, "What emergency could I have that I wouldn't just want to call you?"

Every emergency between the ages of fifteen through twenty-five, actually.

And I share this idea with other parents in my community. At cocktail parties, I say things like, "Well, what you really don't want is for your kid to attempt suicide because they failed a chemistry test and are afraid to tell you."

I am a very strange cocktail party guest.

Need help now?

Say yes first, then negotiate. No, I am not an MBA, thank goodness. But if you are, your negotiating skills might not be helping at home. To be clear, I am saying totally capitulate *first*, then negotiate. Why? When you say no, a teenager's brain goes into fight-or-flight mode, as though they are in mortal danger. This takes over their entire brain and shuts down rational thought.

The fight-or-flight response is controlled by the amygdala. The amygdala is very powerful, but it's also small. Luckily, most of the brain is devoted to thought and contemplation, even in teenagers. After you have said yes and they are out of fight-or-flight, you can have a productive conversation.

Here's an example of how this can work. When he was sixteen, our older son asked if he could drive five friends to a cabin in the mountains for a long weekend. Yikes! Talk about fight-or-flight! That plan had so many problems that we had to turn off our own amygdalae, first! But we said yes and proceeded to negotiate the terms. We got down to a smaller group, for only two nights, with at least one adult in the house at all times, and an adult in the car for any drive longer than a jaunt to the ice cream store.

. . .

I look at my schedule. My next patient had better get here—she missed her last appointment, and I'm worried. A missed appointment is a red flag, but the phone calls I've been getting are even more concerning. Academic advising has been calling about missed exams, and her roommates have been calling about missed meals. As far as I can tell, she's not leaving her room.

So, when she's about five minutes late, I give her a call to see if she's on her way. No answer. When she's fifteen minutes late, I call her again. Still no answer.

This reminds me of something I learned in residency, in addition to several antiquated theories of psychotherapy that are pretty useless in real-world situations. Believe it or not, we spent quite a bit of time talking about whether to call a patient who missed an appointment. This seems insane to me now, but I can remember sitting in a classroom of psychiatry residents discussing whether this was a good idea. For an hour. On more than one occasion. I honestly can't remember the arguments, just a general feeling that the entire conversation was completely patronizing and defied logic.

I did my best to be a dutiful resident, but kept circling back to a fundamental question: What's the worst that could happen? My patient might think I care about them? I have never understood how that could possibly be bad, so I guess everyone else at my residency was just smarter or something. They probably even understood psychoanalytic theory.

So, if I happen to be worried about a patient for whatever reason, I call them. The worst thing that will happen is that they won't pick up.

This girl didn't pick up, twice.

Now I'm in a bind, because I am quite worried about her, and other people are, too. Roommates call us all the time, but the advising office is too busy to call unless they are seriously concerned. I need to do more than just worry, but what? When a student lives on campus, we have options. There is a whole network of supports in place in the residences. Students are barely aware this system exists unless it's needed. If this particular student lived in a dorm, I could make one or two calls, and someone would be knocking on her door in about fifteen minutes. This is one of the reasons I choose to work at BU—I have the systemic backup I need to do my work effectively, which makes it a lot easier to sleep at night.

But this student lives off campus. Now, if your child is about to leave for college and you have the good fortune of meeting me at a cocktail party, you might ask for some last-minute advice. I will have a lot to say, but if it's clear we only have a couple of minutes, I will simply tell you not to let your child live off campus. There are a lot of reasons for this, but the main one is, if a student is having a mental health crisis, I prefer to be able to find them.

I look up the student's demographic profile. She has an off-campus address in the next town, which means a well-being check requires calling the police. Not everyone loves having the police show up at their door, and I don't think this case rises to that level anyway. Luckily, she has an emergency contact on file—her mom.

So I call her mom and explain the situation. The student wasn't doing well the last time I saw her and has now missed two appointments in a row. My office is getting concerned calls. Her mom listens for a while, asks a couple of questions, and is quiet. Then she asks:

"What do you think I should do?"

You're probably thinking, *Obvious question!* But I was totally unprepared! I had no idea how to respond. Obviously, nothing in residency prepared me to handle this—good grief! We only had time to discuss whether to call people, not how to handle their questions! I had no idea how a psychiatrist should answer a question like that, so I answered as a mom:

"I think you should get on a plane and come check on her."

And maybe I should get a kickback from the airlines or something, because when I tell a parent to get on a plane, they invariably do.

CHAPTER EIGHT

Parenting—A Grab Bag

I ran into a student on the street. Not with my car! Although, frankly, that would be quite easy. When I drive to work, the hardest part of my commute is dodging all the students! Good grief, if I make it to my desk without committing involuntary vehicular manslaughter, it's a great start to the day!

That's right, college students can't cross the street. It's honestly one of the requirements for getting into any college, not just BU. Here's how it works. Small children have very poor impulse control, and very little understanding of traffic, so they have to hold hands with an adult at all times. Their judgment and situational awareness gradually improve over time, corresponding with the maturation of their brain's frontal lobe. Most children can reliably cross the street by around third or fourth grade, though usually still with a watchful adult. Fifth grade is peak street-crossing. They walk when they have the light and they stay in the crosswalk, even if they don't think you're watching.

After fifth grade, there's a decline. It starts with not waiting for the light, then progresses to jaywalking. By the time they're sophomores in high school, they generally wander into the street without paying attention at all, which is how you know they're almost ready for college.

So, when I said I ran into a student in the street, I definitely should have clarified! Well this is the second time I've run into a student on the street, metaphorically. The first time, I avoided eye contact and walked by. Because I am rude or socially awkward? No, because this is what I was taught.

This was the sort of thing we had lengthy conversations about in residency—what to do if you saw a patient in public. A topic about as worth discussing as whether to call someone who missed an appointment. Essentially there was this idea that by even smiling or nodding at a patient in public, you were somehow compromising their confidentiality. As if there weren't a hundred other ways they could have known you, or as if it were completely unreasonable to be polite to another human being.

Anyway, I forget the reasons, or maybe I never fully understood them, but you were not supposed to acknowledge a patient in public. In my residency years, I was in a huge city, so these conversations were mostly theoretical, as all the most heated arguments are. In my hospital years, it was also easy. My patients would typically not recognize me outside the hospital context.

So, the first time I encountered a BU student who was also my patient on the street, I didn't make eye contact. I didn't make eye contact even though I had spent hours with this person, and they were clearly looking at me. This felt wrong in every fiber in my body, so I decided not to do it again, even if that is somehow wrong. I'll act like a human, and deal with the aftermath if it upsets someone.

So, when I run into this student on the street, I say hello. He clearly wants to talk to me, so I stop. He wants to thank me for some advice I've given. "Dr. Ross, you know what really helped me? You told me to leave the house fifteen minutes earlier. It's really made a difference!"

Wait, what?! Leave fifteen minutes early? This is someone I spent hours with, over a semester or so. Obsessive Compulsive Disorder. People with OCD often have trouble getting places on time. They have to stop, check, go back, and stop and check again. Anyway, we had done quite a bit of work together. I had introduced the concept of Exposure and Response Prevention and referred him to a therapist specializing in OCD. He was also taking medication. But still, he was having trouble getting places on time because of all the checking, and the lateness was becoming an issue.

During this time my own kids were quite small, and I was reading a lot of parenting books. They mostly weren't that helpful. But one book suggested waking up fifteen minutes earlier if you are consistently having trouble getting your family out the door. I couldn't believe how helpful it was! I had my morning routine down, but if something went wrong it led to frustration, which led to, well, more things going wrong. But by waking up fifteen minutes earlier, I had time to handle things that went wrong! So there was no frustration! So . . . I may have thrown this idea out there because he was having trouble getting places on time. And now he's stopping me on the sidewalk to thank me.

You're having trouble getting places on time? Leave earlier. This sums up what he learned from me.

At least it helped him.

▪ ▪ ▪

Later that morning, I'm in my office talking to someone who is suicidal, which is how I spend a significant portion of the day. The phone rings, and it's Mitzi.

Mitzi. I guess the best way to describe her is to say that she is like a stray dog who wandered into your life and you're not quite sure how you got her but now she's your family and she would do anything for you. This happens a lot with dogs, but not so often with people. In Mitzi's case, she just sort of helps me with anything that happens to come up. She helps me not just because my office is right next to her desk, although that's also true. It's because she helps everyone. She helps people all day long even if she's too busy. She says she considers it her job, but she also helps when it's not her job. I secretly think that she helps so much because she knows the secret of helping. Which is that helping makes you happy, whether or not it's your job.

She also knows things, so you have to answer when she calls, which is practically never. This is because usually, whatever it is, she figures out how to fix it herself.

But this time, Mitzi sounds kind of panicked because my nanny is on the phone sounding kind of panicked, so it might be a terrible emergency worth interrupting talking to a suicidal person. So I take the call from my nanny, who is in a panic, and I immediately assume something terrible has happened.

And it has.

The lizard has gone missing. This actually is terrible. Not because my son is crying, but because this means the lizard could possibly come creeping into my bed later that night. It would be pretty easy to get swept up in this panic.

By now I've realized that while my nanny is in a panic, which led to the absurd situation of being on the phone with him instead of being present with a suicidal student, this is not the kind of panic that means there is an emergency. This is the kind of panic that just means it's my nanny's first week and he's probably worried about his job, and he's definitely worried about my son, which is completely endearing.

So this is not actually an emergency. It's important to my nanny and son at the moment, but not in the long run. But suicide is, and I'm on the phone while there is a suicidal person sitting next to me. I have to say something to calm my nanny down without the student next to me catching on. So I say in my mom voice: "It's probably going to be okay."

I'm not sure that's true, but I take a quick inventory of risk factors, and none of them apply to the lizard situation, so that will have to do.

And I turn my attention back to the suicidal person in my office like none of this happened, because . . . they are probably not okay.

This story has a happy ending because the lizard reappeared and the patient got better. Well, I would've been fine if the lizard hadn't been found because I really don't like lizards. But my son and nanny were happy.

And the lizard didn't come creeping into my bed that night.

▪ ▪ ▪

Lizard or no, I wasn't able to sleep that night. When they were little, my children had an extremely well-organized system to make sure I never got a complete night's sleep. It was my daughter's turn, and I was up for most of the night with her.

The next morning, a student in my office is crying about a breakup. Seriously? I haven't slept because my toddler was in a mood, and she's talking about a breakup? I do enough of an assessment to verify that this truly is just a breakup, not a sign of something serious, and settle in feeling sorry for myself, because this is a waste of my time.

Is it a problem to consult a psychiatrist for a breakup? It can be, if it's truly the only issue. Grief is a normal part of the human condition, a normal process. Encouraging professional consultation for ordinary grief contributes to a general idea in our culture that emotions are mostly pathological.

At least, this is my opinion if I haven't slept or didn't have time for breakfast.

On this day, I think about my father instead. When I was about twelve years old, he got a call on Christmas Day, when we were celebrating. He immediately took the call and was gone for twenty minutes or so. When he came back, I asked what the call was about. "Oh, somebody with a broken thumb."

"A broken thumb?" I answered. "That doesn't sound important enough to bother you on Christmas Day." He gave me a look that . . . Let's just call it a look I have never forgotten.

"It is," he replied gently, "if you are the one with the broken thumb."

I pull myself together and listen to the student.

At least, I try to look like I'm listening.

▪ ▪ ▪

In walks a sad young woman who is getting used to living on her own, which is not really a mental health problem but is something our office encounters a lot. So, I start talking about things that help people adjust to new situations, like decorating your room *just so* and leaving your dorm as much as possible so you have opportunities to meet people. And in these conversations, I usually talk about exercise, because exercise helps with sleep and anxiety, and is also a fun way to meet people. So I bring it up with her.

"I can't exercise," she replies.

"Why not?"

She explains that she has a back injury and can't do most forms of exercise. This seems odd to me, because in med school most back injuries I learned about involved middle-aged men and hard physical labor. But she has a back injury significant enough that she can't do most any exercise, which would otherwise be good for her. So I keep asking.

She was a gymnast. She loved it. Trained every day after school for hours. But also had a series of injuries, many quite serious. She always made a brave comeback. Until she didn't.

Many mental health professionals are quite skeptical of most organized sports. Before working with college students myself, I thought this was mostly because of eating disorders.

Eating disorders, remember? Like the model. Well, let me tell you something. There are lots of ways to make sure a teenager gets an eating disorder, if that's what you're going for. Modeling is probably the most efficient, but the overall numbers are small. Gymnastics is not quite as effective as modeling for creating eating disorders, but it's still quite effective, and the numbers of little girls doing gymnastics are quite huge, so if you add it all up . . . that's a lot of eating disorders. Ballet is probably somewhere in between modeling and gymnastics, if you're interested.

I knew I was likely to see many eating disorders in a college setting. I prepared myself for my gymnast's story. But I was not at all prepared for the girl in my office. She doesn't have an eating disorder at all. That would've been quite likely to resolve with treatment. She has the injuries of a lifelong manual laborer. Because of gymnastics.

It wasn't just an unlucky injury. It was an injury that came with warning signs. The previous injuries. Gymnastics gets more dangerous the better you get, so the injuries also get more serious. It's a slippery slope. Closer and closer until . . . you just slip. But then you have a serious back problem for the rest of your life. And in her case, it happened when she was fourteen. And now she's eighteen. And still can't even do basic exercise. Or even comfortably carry a backpack.

Where were the grown-ups? Maybe their hair was in their eyes, or they were just trying to get some work done. They didn't realize their daughter was on a slippery slope and she had gotten too close to the edge. She had gotten so good. That was obvious, because now she could do the dangerous tricks.

Maybe they tried to get her to stop but her coach was telling her she was good, though honestly, she could stand to lose a pound or two, or at the very least not develop a healthy body. But most likely her parents didn't try very hard to get her to stop because *they didn't know how important it was.*

Most things start small, even eating disorders, maybe especially eating disorders. Early on it's quite easy to intervene. But after a certain point a slippery slope becomes quite difficult to recover from, as with more serious eating disorders, which are quite difficult to treat, and also quite miserable. Slippery slopes are difficult to navigate, as a certain skier found out the hard way.

But sometimes it's hard to know if you're even on one. And in this case, I think the family didn't. No one wants their daughter's life to be ruined by a gymnastics accident. It was bad luck, right? Was it? Some of the previous injuries were also quite serious; they were red flags. And the tricks were getting more dangerous. Was it really an accident, or just inevitable?

That's the thing about slippery slopes. You have to intervene before it's too late. That's why pediatricians never let their own kids do gymnastics.

When you think about accidents, you have to wonder if it might be the kind of accident that is inevitable at Deer Valley. Too many people who are not prepared for how steep the slope is, or how slippery. Not everyone will be crashed into by an orthodontist, but some will, and you don't want it to be someone in your family.

For me an easy shortcut is honestly just to stay away from Deer Valley.

CHAPTER NINE

No, You're Not Old-Fashioned. Marijuana Really Is Bad for Young People.

The next student is a little depressed. Actually, pretty depressed. He's apathetic, uninterested in anything—he's more or less checked out. Is it just depression, or the prodrome of psychosis? Either way, his frequent marijuana use probably isn't helping. He's here to get back on track, which is a good sign, but there are also some bad signs. Multiple relatives with schizophrenia, which is a life-changing mental illness characterized by chronic psychosis. He's at very high risk.

During this time period, we were completely panicked about marijuana. I mean, *clinicians* were panicked about it, not the people using it, though quite a few of them were having panic attacks. Why were we panicked? Because all the students kept getting into our break room and stealing all our snacks!

No, we were panicked because marijuana was becoming more socially acceptable and more readily available, and a generation of young people had even grown up with the idea that it was medicine. But there was very good data that it was (and is) bad for the developing brain, including sometimes causing a psychosis that is difficult to treat. Now, just about everyone knows that marijuana can cause many other problems, like panic attacks, cognitive problems, lack of motivation, apathy, and generally eating too much Ben & Jerry's, as well as a surprisingly persistent aroma. However, all that stuff is mostly reversible. We were worried about the psychosis, and no one knew what the numbers were going to look like.

That number has turned out to be much smaller than we feared, though I personally see at least one or two patients a year with marijuana-induced psychosis. This can take up to a year to resolve and sometimes requires longer term treatment with antipsychotic medication. Luckily there hasn't been a tsunami of young people with psychosis, mostly just a tsunami of kids with problems that are easily reversible by quitting. But it was hard to know this at the time because marijuana, like guns, was not allowed to be studied. Studies, for people like me, are how we know things, as opposed to just thinking. You are aware by now that I am suspicious of thinking, because our brains are naturally overconfident.

I find it a little problematic that I don't have studies on some very important issues in my field. Like, whether it is possible for marijuana to ruin a brain forever, and if so, whose. It's impossible for me to know if an individual such as the young man in my office is at risk. This means it's also impossible for you to know if the teenager at your dining room table is at risk. So I tell every teenager I know about this dilemma: Marijuana is low risk for most people but extremely high risk for others, and there's no way to know which group you're in.

Now, for most people over twenty-five with no history of addiction, the risk is quite low. So, if someone is really curious about marijuana, I encourage them to wait until their late twenties, by which time they will probably have noticed how bad it smells. But for someone with a family or personal history of any form of psychosis, my recommendation is never, ever, ever.

Need help now?

Set the right example. Specifically, don't use marijuana. Yes, you. Most of the issues I deal with are easily preventable. Marijuana is an important underlying cause of many of the common problems in my office, as well as some serious-but-rare conditions. I spend a lot of time and energy steering young people toward making better choices. It is painstaking and time-consuming work, but it's worth it. But there is one line of reasoning that is impenetrable: "My dad uses marijuana, so it must be fine." They will never believe my words over your actions—it's as simple as that. So do your kid a favor and stop.

November—Problems, Sleep, and Sleep Problems

CHAPTER TEN

A Decade of Medical Training Boils Down to This: You're Tired? Sleep More.

If it's November, everyone is probably losing it. By everyone, I mean all my colleagues. It's the most hectic month of the year in my office. Why? Sleep deprivation, mostly. Students simply refuse to get adequate rest, and ten weeks of sleep deprivation reliably leads to various psychiatric symptoms. Students think they're depressed, or have ADHD, or maybe it's mono or some other mystery illness. Either way, they find their way to my office in huge numbers.

On a particularly busy morning, Mitzi pulls me aside to whisper a heads-up about the drop-in that has been added to my schedule. Sometimes this means she wants me to take a breath before encountering a particularly traumatic situation. Sometimes, it's the opposite: She needs me to keep a straight face. Today, it's the latter. The girl in my schedule started having a panic attack in the laundry room because—she didn't know how to do laundry. There were other people around who seemed to know what they were doing, but she felt too humiliated to ask for help . . . and she had a panic attack.

Laundry? Seriously? It's *November*! (No wonder it's such an emergency!)

Mitzi gives me a look that means I am definitely not allowed to invite the girl over to my house for extra practice. Rats! Okay, time for some breathing exercises or guided imagery, followed by some general problem-solving and practice asking for help, as well as identifying people in her life who may have the necessary skills. The latter is easy, because it's literally anybody.

Is she an outlier? Nope. We see the laundry skill–less in our office almost every year. Please bear in mind that my colleagues and I have anywhere from two to ten years of postgraduate education marshaled for this particular assist.

But it is *November*, so maybe she is a *tiny* bit of an outlier.

▪ ▪ ▪

The next student isn't here to discuss laundry, though based on his appearance, it's not a bad idea. He starts talking. His motivation has been kind of low, and he's not as interested in his classes as usual. He's putting things off, feeling generally apathetic, and getting sick frequently. He can't concentrate very well, and his schoolwork is taking longer than it should. He's also craving carbs. He's wondering if he's a little depressed or maybe developing ADHD.

I ask him how much sleep he has been getting.

"Six hours a night, but that's enough for me."

I wish I had a dollar for every time I have had this conversation. A student spends twenty minutes describing the symptoms of chronic sleep deprivation, then confidently tells me they are getting enough sleep. I *love* it when this happens. I mean, four years of med school and four years of residency for an intervention that boils down to: You're tired, so sleep more.

This student is obviously impervious to common sense, so I'm going to have to expound. I have done this so many times that I have several ways to describe the importance of sleep, and the impact of sleep deprivation.

I begin by telling him that his sleep requirement is probably eight to nine hours per night, and review that sleep deprivation is cumulative. He has probably been missing at least two hours of sleep per night, which adds up to about two missed *nights* of sleep per week. Multiply this by the number of weeks that have passed in the current semester and that gives you . . . he has missed a lot of sleep.

I ask him if he has heard of Bank of America, which he has. Now I get to explain debt, even though I am not in the School of Management. (It's my office, so I get to use whatever metaphor I choose!) If you borrow five bucks from Bank of America, you owe them five bucks. If you do this twenty times you owe them $100. Bank of America isn't going to say, "don't worry about it, just pay us back $70." You have to pay back the whole $100, and everyone understands this. Well, you probably also owe some interest, but that's beyond the scope of this metaphor. Go to the School of Management if you want to learn about that.

The point is, you have to pay back every dollar, and sleep works the same way. So if you have massive sleep debt, you won't feel better after a night or two. I have found that I have to explain this to people, or they go get two nights of good sleep and tell me they're still having the same problems. Bank of America isn't too impressed if you've only paid back $20.

I give him the homework of sleeping nine hours per night for the next two weeks, with a follow-up appointment to tell me how he's doing. This is homework that I would've loved in college, or really any time in my adult life, but students sometimes don't like it. They have to stay up late procrastinating with their friends, and sleeping more would interfere with that. Besides, more sleep isn't *sciency* enough; it doesn't feel like the kind of advice you would get from a real doctor.

The student is pretty impressed with my math, but he still doesn't believe he needs more than six hours of sleep per night, in spite of what his body is telling him, not to mention my professional opinion, which is the whole purpose of the appointment. He keeps pushing. Maybe he needs some labs drawn or something. Or maybe some kind of medication. Or maybe some kind of specialist.

I resist the urge to explain to him that a psychiatrist *is* a specialist. (That's right! Psychiatry is a brain specialty. Just ask any neurologist, and they will argue with you. I mean they will agree with you.)

At this point I'm getting exasperated, because I really do have eight years of medical training, and this really is the solution to his problem, and I could really use a nap myself. It's just not the solution he wants to hear. Besides, he's been acculturated to believe that sleep is optional, and he has some friends who genuinely need less sleep than he does.

"Look," I say, "sleep is as important as breathing."

Oh no, what have I done? That was a totally ridiculous thing to say: I've overstated my case and now he's never going to take me seriously . . . but his eyes have gone wide, and I finally have his attention . . . I should probably clarify that I was using hyperbole to make a point because otherwise that sounds insane . . . he's expecting me to keep talking . . .

"Look, sleep and breathing are bodily functions that are so important that evolution has put them under both voluntary and involuntary control. You can hold your breath for a while, like kids playing in a pool. But eventually, the urge to breathe becomes so powerful that it is almost irresistible. If you continue to resist, you pass out, and your body starts to breathe for you. Sleep is the same way. You can resist it to a point, but eventually your body will claim it whenever it can—in class, riding the bus, even driving. No other behaviors are like this, even behaviors that are essential to survival, like eating. It is very hard to resist food when you are hungry, but it is never truly under involuntary control."

Where on earth did that come from? I took a totally ridiculous position and doubled down on it. Now he's definitely going to think I'm not a specialist. He probably also thinks I don't understand interest. I should've called in sick today. What a mess!

But that's not the response I'm getting from him. I finally have his attention.

He says he's going to try the two-week thing . . . and he makes another appointment.

In retrospect I'm not sure if it's funnier that I cooked up the *sleep is as important as breathing* metaphor or that he ran with it. But what's even funnier than both of those things is . . . how many times I have used it since. And it always gets their attention. Boy, does it get their attention.

Lots of people somehow believe that sleep is optional, or maybe weak, but they have mostly gotten the message on breathing.

My goal is to help young people take control of their lives, mostly by helping them make better decisions. To do this, I have to get their attention, even if it occasionally means stretching the truth.

So sleep is as important as breathing, people. You heard it here first. But if it's a question on an exam, please don't use that as your answer.

CHAPTER ELEVEN

If the Internet Says It's ADHD, It's Probably Not.

The next student hasn't checked in yet, and he's already several minutes late. I check his profile and see that he missed an appointment with one of my colleagues last week, so he hasn't been assessed yet. I assume he's not in class (he scheduled the appointment after all), and I have long since abandoned the idea that calling a patient might be harmful in some way that I never understood. So I give him a call.

He totally forgot about the appointment . . . which he scheduled yesterday. He's deeply apologetic, frankly to a self-flagellating degree, and he wants to come in right away to be evaluated for Attention-Deficit/Hyperactivity Disorder, though he just uses the familiar nickname, ADHD.

This is quite a difficult diagnosis to make in a college setting. Because of the lengthy lists of diagnostic criteria? Of course not! Good grief, I don't bother with those, but probably not for the reason you suspect. (Much more coming on that!) In the case of ADHD, the diagnostic criteria are quite good, but there's a problem: Anyone can just go online and memorize them. You know who's really good at going online and memorizing stuff? College students! So any number of people make an appointment and look up the criteria online then come to my office and tell me they have ADHD.

If a student comes to their appointment *on time* and tells me they think they have ADHD, reciting the list of symptoms, they definitely don't have it. Not a chance! No one with true ADHD would bother with all of that!

They usually have *something*, most often an anxiety disorder. Sometimes they just use too much pot, which is quite easy to diagnose because in addition to advanced medical training, I have a nose. Sometimes they don't have any diagnosis at all; they're just somewhat overextended and very human. Maybe they heard that spending an hour with me is one of the perks of attending BU. Who can blame them?

No, ADHD is a very difficult diagnosis to make because people with untreated ADHD can't get into the office for an appointment!

This is how it goes. If someone has an appointment for an ADHD evaluation, and they show up on time, they probably don't have the diagnosis. (Although if they show up on time, at least I can fully assess them.) If they show up five to ten minutes late, or if they show up on time after missing a previous appointment, there's a reasonable chance they have ADHD. And if they fully miss a second appointment or arrive more than twenty minutes late to any appointment, they almost definitely have ADHD. I learned about this in statistics: It's called pretest probability.

So the pretest probability of ADHD in the student I have on the phone is close to 100 percent, because he was in the process of missing his second appointment, but I can't diagnose someone who has never been in my office. So this diagnosis is very hard to make!

I ask him to run right over to the office, and he does. Obviously, there's no time to review the full diagnostic criteria, and he hasn't memorized them anyway, so I cut to the chase and ask how many all-nighters he has pulled. Now, most college students have stayed up all night working on an academic project at least once, but they pretty quickly figure out that it's extremely unpleasant. So, in general, by their second semester of college, students develop an organizational system to avoid getting into that situation. I'm not saying the all-nighter is essential to learning basic organization, but it's a very effective teacher.

Not all all-nighters are voluntary. I had to stay up all night routinely during residency, just like most other doctors in training. Psychiatry residents don't take overnight call as often as other specialties, but they do have to act compassionate during the process, which is psychologically draining. But it was obviously completely necessary, because being exhausted and stressed out is the best way to learn. Wait, that doesn't sound right. Huh. However, those all-nighters *did* teach me a little about how awful it must be to live with untreated ADHD, so maybe it wasn't a total waste.

Whether or not I learned anything in residency, I am now responsible for assessing a patient for ADHD, in a short amount of time. Luckily, I know the shortcut of just asking about all-nighters. He's doing it routinely, not because he enjoys it . . . because it's the only way he ever gets anything done. He needs the adrenalin of a crisis to be able to focus, so he bounces from crisis to crisis. This is a stressful way to live, and he is not learning well. The young people I meet are often brilliant and have often progressed quite far academically in spite of untreated ADHD, but they hit a wall eventually. That's when they turn to me. It's impossible to complete a PhD dissertation on a series of all-nighters. Trust me, I've met a number of people who have tried.

Once the diagnosis is established, it's time to talk about treatment. You have a head start here, because you've already learned that nothing about humans makes sense. Just like everything else, people who don't need medication for ADHD think they do, and people who do need medication for ADHD . . . are often reluctant to try it.

He's concerned about the available treatments for ADHD, because he's heard they sometimes make students stay up all night. He's also concerned that the medications in question are *controlled substances*, which he's heard can mess up your life. I observe that he's already routinely staying up all night, and his life is already a mess. The public perception is that medications for ADHD make students strung out and sleep deprived; the reality is that these medications make their lives more boring. They just do their work during the day, so they can relax with friends in the evening, and sleep at night. Just like living at your mom's house.

Luckily once a student like this starts medication, their life gets a lot easier.

Wrong again! Why? Because we have a system that makes it almost impossible for patients to fill prescriptions for *controlled substances*. There are tons of rules that have to be followed *just so,* including a very particular timeframe. It's much worse in very blue states, but it's basically a nationwide thing. Essentially, we have a system that puts up extraordinary logistical obstacles for people who struggle with organization, to access the medication that helps them with their organizational problems. Are you following? Of course not! It's incomprehensible!

Need help now?

It's probably not ADHD. ADHD really does exist, but your teenager probably doesn't have it, no matter what the internet says. Lots of teenagers oversleep, live in messy rooms, leave their shoes and backpack in the middle of the kitchen floor, and forget their keys. Most of them grow out of it, with or without your nagging, though the nagging makes you feel like you're doing something. Unless you're getting phone calls from their school, it's probably not ADHD. Sorry, you just have to live with it until their frontal lobe matures a little more.

CHAPTER TWELVE

No, Caffeine Is Not the Solution. It's Just Another Problem!

I arrive one morning to find an Incident Report on my desk, which usually means a student has been taken to the emergency room overnight. We don't always hear about emergency room visits if a student goes on their own, but if a BU-affiliated adult is involved, our good friends at BUPD write an Incident Report. Those guys could write quite an interesting book, if their collective reports are any indication.

I'm on triage so it's my turn, and I review the Incident Report to see if I need to follow up. The student was taken to the hospital with cardiac symptoms, which you might be surprised to hear most likely *is* my problem. I read on. Yup, caffeine and Adderall, heart rate in the 140s when the EMTs arrived.

I look at my watch. As a rule, it's a mistake to review Incident Reports before 11 A.M., because if the relevant student needs a follow-up phone call, they are most likely asleep. However, if the BUPD time stamp is 3 A.M. or after, there's a good chance that the student is *still awake* when I arrive at the office in the morning. Especially if they've used enough caffeine and stimulants to earn an ambulance ride.

So I call her, and she picks up. She's crying, so I ask if she can come into the office. Between tears she tells me she can't possibly come in, because she has an exam in two hours that she has been studying for all night. She doesn't sound like someone who is going to take an exam in two hours, and we have already established that she hasn't been studying all night.

Students inevitably think missing an exam is the end of the world, but last I checked, it's not. I encourage her to come to the office; we can craft an email to her professor, and she can arrange an alternative when she's feeling better. (I don't remember how we handled stuff like this when I was an email-less college student; maybe missing an exam really *was* the end of the world back then.)

She's in my office fifteen minutes later, still crying. She's never stayed up all night, been to an emergency room, or seen a psychiatrist before, so she's honestly a typical college freshman. Here's what she tells me: She had a paper to write and an exam to prepare for, so she planned to stay up pretty late. When her usual bedtime rolled around, she was tired, so she had a cup of coffee, and then another. A couple of hours later she had an energy drink. A couple of hours after *that* she was still feeling kind of tired. Her roommate told her that Adderall works quickly, so she took one of those. After another forty-five minutes her heart was pounding out of her chest, and she thought she was going to die.

Here's what happened. Caffeine from coffee reaches peak efficacy after three or four hours, not immediately. (That *immediate* energy boost is most likely from walking to the break room and chatting with your colleagues, as well as placebo effect and sugar if you use it.) Energy drinks act faster, because they are designed to be taken as a shot, not sipped. (Just as a shot of vodka is more intoxicating than a glass of wine, in spite of having the same alcohol content.) Adderall acts faster still, because that is what it's designed to do. So she took three stimulants with different pharmacokinetic properties, all of which peaked in her system at about the same time.

Pharmacokinetics: That's the science that describes how long after ingestion a drug becomes active, how long it lasts, and how quickly it is eliminated. People often ask me how a given medication works, but they rarely ask about its pharmacokinetic profile. For a psychiatrist, that latter is just as important to understand, maybe even more important. The girl in my office didn't think she was doing anything dangerous, and she would have been right if she had taken the same doses of caffeine and stimulants in the opposite order. (Well, taking her roommate's *prescription* medication was still a *tiny* bit dangerous, but I don't need to scold her because she's learned the hard way.)

It's the same with sleep meds. (You can call them hypnotics, or sedatives, or sleeping pills, but in my office pretty much everyone says "sleep meds.") Turns out it's pretty important to take your morning plans into account before taking something for sleep. Or even afternoon plans. Once my nanny was late for school pickup at 2:30 P.M. The reason? She took a dose of melatonin at 3 A.M., and slept for nearly twelve hours straight. She is a lovely person and has gone on to become a mental health professional. But even at the time, I could hardly be mad because this is such a common mistake.

One morning on triage I meet a young woman who's mortified that she slept through an exam. She set an alarm for 7 A.M., but didn't wake up until 10 A.M. She asks me if there's something wrong with her. I do a little investigating and discover that she has a prescription sleep med that she takes on a regular basis. I ask when she normally takes it. She answers but adds that on the night in question she took it later than usual because she was up late studying—around 1 A.M. Oops. Based on the pharmacokinetic profile of the prescription she has, 10 A.M. is about when you would expect her to wake up. So good news, there's nothing wrong with her at all!

When I'm discussing sleep meds, I always tell people to think about their twenty-four-hour clock and take the medication nine hours before they plan to wake up the next morning. Expect it to take up to an hour to start working, then allow eight hours for a full night's sleep. (I also advise them not to take any sedative for the first time if they have anything important the following morning, because everyone is different, as a certain insomnia-suffering nanny learned.)

She considers this, then asks if there is a shorter-acting option, for nights when she stays up later. I'm kind of impressed with how quickly she's taken to pharmacokinetics, but in the case of sleep, the eight hours is kind of the point. She explains that she sometimes has time for a long nap during the day. I've heard this argument before, so I gently explain that when it comes to sleep, five plus three does not equal eight. (I *know*! Engineering majors really look at me askance when I say *that*!)

Lemme Go!

Leave **your phone at home.** Tired of arguing with your parents about their use of location tracking? Tired of hearing that they're paying for your phone, so you're leaving it on? (No, you're not the first family to have this argument; you're not even the thousandth. Sorry to disappoint.) So leave it at home! They won't be able to track you. What are they going to do, insist that you carry your phone with you at all times? Seriously?!

CHAPTER THIRTEEN

Where Did This Culture of Overscheduling and Sleep Deprivation Come from Anyway? The Parenting Pandemic.

The next student in my office is also here for symptoms of sleep deprivation. This is how a lot of my days go. If you meet me at a cocktail party and ask me about my job, and I am in a certain mood, I will answer, "Mostly, I spend my days trying to get young people to sleep more." I believe it's getting pretty clear that I am a strange cocktail party guest. But in the case of young people and mental health, it's honestly the biggest issue.

So anyway, I begin explaining to him that he needs to sleep eight hours a night, maybe more. He interrupts me to tell me that sleep is a waste of time.

Oh no. I forgot to mention that he is in the School of Management. He probably knows about compound interest, but he most likely doesn't know the difference between spending and wasting. You see, in the School of Management they learn about two columns—spending and earning. They don't learn the difference between spending and wasting, because with money, it's the same.

But humans are not cash registers, and spending and wasting are not the same. Humans need a third column. Take carpool, for example. A lot of people think it's a waste of time, but it's not. Well, it can be, like if you arrive for pickup thirty minutes before practice ends because the coach posted the wrong time. But mostly, it's *spending* time, because this is when children will talk to you. Technically, they mostly talk to their friends, but it's still how you learn what's going on. You have already learned that it's an excellent time to talk to teenagers about child exploitation. Anyway, carpool is mostly *spending* time. Organizing carpool is sort of a gray area. Definitely a bit of a drag, but involves interacting with other moms, so it's a wash.

So I taught him the difference between spending and wasting, which he hasn't learned at the School of Management. I should say *Questrom*. It changed its name overnight, which was one of the more remarkable things I have ever witnessed. One day it was School of Management, and the next day it was Questrom. And that's what everyone had to say all the time. If you accidentally said *School of Management*, even in the privacy of your own office, everyone would hush and look around like you said something deeply offensive. So now we all call it Questrom. Imagine if that kind of discipline went into changing names that actually are offensive!

It reminds me of my town, which recently changed the name of an elementary school. It took three years! The first year was mostly about making people understand why the old name was problematic. Once people knew the story, they were mostly shocked. Then there was a year of a rather dry interim name, so we would all get really bored, and therefore motivated to learn the new name. The third year was to give us plenty of time to learn how to pronounce the new name, which I can attest was necessary. So I know all about name changes.

The student in my office wasn't at BU during the name change, so he's not terribly impressed that I remember to say *Questrom*. But now he understands the difference between spending and wasting and agrees that he will start prioritizing eight hours of sleep per night. Based on when he typically has to get up in the morning to get to class, that means going to sleep at 11 P.M., which he will start . . . tomorrow.

Why not tonight? He explains that he has a paper due at midnight, which obviously means he will be submitting it at 11:59 P.M., after which he will have to start all his other homework. Oh no, I've already spent a lot of time covering spending vs. wasting, and now I'm going to have to teach him about sleep-friendly policies. He looks at me like I'm crazy. (Thinking about that now, he may have had a point.)

Here's a good example of a sleep-friendly policy. The gyms in my town close at 10 P.M. Actually, the lights turn off at 10 P.M., so practices have to wrap up by 9:45 P.M. so no one gets stuck in the dark. This means for the six months of the year when bad weather precludes outdoor activities, everyone has to finish their sports practices by 10 P.M. Otherwise there would be practices from 10–11 P.M., and 11–12 P.M. . . . honestly, there would probably be practices all night.

Why would people otherwise be holding youth sports practices all night at all the local gyms? I guess this would be a good time to tell you about the parenting pandemic, in case you haven't heard of it. It hasn't been covered by the newspapers, because when it comes to mental health the newspapers mostly just report on all the ways that Mark Zuckerberg has been causing a crisis. It's pretty easy to put these articles together—just cut and paste *mental health* into articles about all the other problems he's supposedly causing. Plus, the paying readership of the remaining major newspapers is significantly implicated in the parenting pandemic, so they would prefer to keep it quiet.

I'm honestly not sure whether to describe the parenting pandemic using the past or present tense, because I don't know if it's still going on. Because there's no way to know if a parenting trend is positive or toxic until about ten years later, when the aftermath starts walking into my office. So maybe don't jump on board parenting trends until they've been established for a generation or so. Because the parenting pandemic has ruined childhood for many kids over the past couple of decades.

Where should I begin? The parenting pandemic was caused by Malcolm Gladwell. Technically, he didn't cause it—he was just the lab leak. (That's sort of his thing: finding an interesting idea and making it contagious.) It started with a researcher who was interested in the development of young musicians. He was trying to understand how many hours of practice it takes to become a virtuoso. And he came up with a number that you have probably heard—10,000 hours.

Sound familiar? The basic idea is, to become Yo-Yo Ma or maybe Derek Jeter, you have to practice a skill for 10,000 hours. Sounds like a lot? You bet! So the sooner you start, the better! It used to be that if a child showed no aptitude for music, his parents would just let him play in the school band to learn the basics of music and develop some teamwork and social skills, and consider their job done. All the better not to have to listen to him practicing his instrument incessantly! But now that the 10,000 hours idea is out there, every parent knows that if their child shows no aptitude for music . . . they have to get him to practice for 10,000 hours! And then they will have Yo-Yo Ma.

But, when a child is very young, it's hard to know if they will be Yo-Yo Ma or Derek Jeter or maybe Serena Williams . . . so better have them do 10,000 hours of each! And for goodness' sake make sure they don't have any unscheduled time to develop friendships or maybe even occasionally be bored. Either of these pursuits could easily let them develop ideas of their own.

What if they are destined to be Albert Einstein? Or any other Nobel Prize winner? You obviously have to make sure they take several dozen AP classes. If they are not on track to take that many APs by approximately third grade, you should get them several hours of tutoring every week. This will have the side effect of ensuring that they don't have any time to build friendships, which will increase the chances of their developing mental health problems. Because every parent knows you can't get into college without a mental health problem! At least, that's how they have been acting for the past two decades.

Parenting trends are highly contagious even when they are not healthy, and the parenting pandemic quickly spread all over the country. I find that it is particularly widespread in communities where everyone is shocked that their teenagers are having mental health crises and standing and shouting that someone should come and do something about it. Your community may be at risk if you hear adults saying things like, "why are our kids so overscheduled?" Let me give you a hint: I have never known a child under the age of fifteen to schedule a single thing.

But obviously you have to stick with the script. Your child isn't going to get into an Ivy unless they are Yo-Yo Ma or Derek Jeter or Serena Williams, so it's better to just demand that someone do something about the mental health crisis in teenagers, like maybe have congressional hearings that blame Mark Zuckerberg.

What do you want, for Mitch McConnell or AOC to come raise your kids?

AOC wasn't available during this stage of the parenting pandemic, because she was too busy being a BU student. That's right—she went to BU. You might not remember that, because now she's successful, which means she probably went to an Ivy. This is a kind of cognitive bias. You believe that Ivy League colleges lead to future success, so you assume successful people went to an Ivy. But in the case of AOC, it is not violating confidentiality to say she went to BU, because it is a matter of the public record. Also, one of my colleagues was in her class.

She never came to my office, because . . . she probably has very good parents. Well, had. I happen to remember a lovely speech in which she mentioned that her father had died, and I remember it well because it made me cry, and crying is very good at making you remember things. Anyway, she seems to be doing fine without me, and I have a lot of respect for her. This is not to say I agree with her on everything, but it's possible to respect and disagree at the same time—I do it all the time. Well, you can't do it in public anymore, but you can do it in the privacy of your own home, and you can also do it in my office. Because my office is confidential.

But one thing AOC and I would probably agree on is that she's not responsible for other people's children. And neither is Mitch McConnell.

So everyone blames everyone else for their teenager's mental health, while they keep driving them harder. Because obviously they have to get into an Ivy. Because otherwise their lives would be ruined and they'd turn out like . . . AOC, I guess. But we can all agree that getting into an Ivy is more important than having a joyful childhood.

Isn't it?

In this book, we are going to be discussing the college admissions process, because of its outsized impact on mental health in young people. Is it the most important factor? No, I don't think so—much more is coming on the major causes of mental health problems in young people. It's not the *magnitude* of the impact, it's the *breadth*: It affects so many young people to some degree. It's sort of like phones. Since they are so widespread, the impact is broad, and there will occasionally be a horror story. I happen to think the impact of the college admissions process on mental health is much more significant than the impact of phones, because that is what I see.

You have probably quickly guessed the college admissions process impacts some people more than others. This is definitely true. There are numerous high schools where the entire culture is driven by it. You know what I am talking about: the highly competitive college prep stress factories that we call elite high schools. This results in a high school culture focused on learning to impress, as opposed to learning. And it also often results in high schools where significant mental health problems are quite common.

In certain communities, it is easy to find a seventh grader who says things like, "I'm going to take Latin in high school because it's going to look better for Yale." Now, everyone knows that Yale doesn't care whether you took Latin; they only care whether your parents went there, and how much money you gave the tennis coach, I mean how good you are at tennis. A thirteen-year-old doesn't know this; they don't even know who they are. Yet they are making decisions to shape their identity to be more appealing to Yale. I find this so deeply disturbing that I don't really know where to begin, so I'm not going to.

In my office we spend a lot of time dealing with the consequences of the parenting pandemic. Young people who are burned out, and don't know who they are. They know who their parents want them to be—they've gotten that message. But they've been driven to achieve, at the expense of knowing who they are, how to take care of themselves, or even if it's worth it. A parenting style that emphasizes achievement at all costs . . . has a cost.

In mental health, some things are not preventable, like bipolar disorder or OCD, and probably some forms of depression. These syndromes affect a relatively small percentage of people, but it would help them a lot if my schedule weren't filled with completely preventable things. Like burned-out eighteen-year-olds. I meet a significant number of young people for whom the only reason for their mental health problem . . . is that they went to high school. This is so obviously wrong that a mommy-track hair-braiding bread-liking lizard-losing happily composting carpool-driving soccer-coaching psychiatrist shouldn't have to write a book about it.

Here's the irony of the parenting pandemic: unless your goal is to raise stressed out kids who hate you, I don't even think it works. I highly doubt that Yo-Yo Ma's mother was standing behind him with a stopwatch and a timesheet, making sure he got his 10,000 hours in. (Although I wish the *New York Times* interviewer had asked!) No, I kind of bet Yo-Yo Ma just loved music. I bet his mom had to pull him away from his instrument to have dinner and get to bed at a reasonable hour. He has had an extremely long career, which implies excellent self-care, which—based on certain stereotypes—he probably didn't learn at Julliard.

What's my evidence that Yo-Yo Ma loved music as a child, and frankly still loves it? You don't need to be Board Certified (a.k.a. certifiable) in psychiatry to know this one. It's simple, even if you've forgotten everything about neuroanatomy, and don't know how to interpret an fMRI. *He always has a smile on his face!* Seriously, find me a picture of Yo-Yo Ma, and I will show you a picture of a happy man. I challenge you to scour the internet for a picture in which he isn't smiling. The man exudes joy.

Here's where modern parents get it wrong. The prevailing attitude is that if you drive your child to be successful like Yo-Yo Ma, they will be happy. But that's backward. Yo-Yo Ma's joy doesn't come from his success; his success came from his joy.

You could argue that I've never met Yo-Yo Ma, so this is all opinion and conjecture. So somebody call him up and ask him. And while you're at it, thank him on my behalf for many wonderful naps.

Luckily, I live in an enlightened town that values the mental health of children and has developed sleep-friendly policies to push back against the worst of the parenting pandemic. Did my town develop a sleep-friendly policy on purpose? Good grief, no! My town can't fix a pothole. In fact, you have to have a 4WD vehicle to get down any street in my neighborhood. But you have to be critical of everyone else's 4WD vehicle because they use more gas, and you care about the environment! (Living in my town is very complicated!) In all fairness, my town did accomplish something once—you may recall that it changed the name of a school, and it only took three years. So no, this particular sleep-friendly policy had to have been an accident. My best guess is that someone set a timer for the gym lights in 1989, and no one knows how to reset it. But until they do, the kids in my town will continue to get to bed at a reasonable hour.

So having a paper due at midnight is a sleep-unfriendly policy. It doesn't affect the professor—she's probably home getting good sleep. She probably also has well-developed executive function, because she is a grown-up. But instead of sleep-friendly policies for college students, we rely on each of them to have the wherewithal to go to bed at a reasonable hour, while living in a highly stimulating environment. This is not a wonderful way of going about things because executive function isn't fully developed until about age twenty-five.

Is this student particularly disorganized? Should we really design policies with him in mind? Isn't it his problem that he left this project until the last possible minute? Don't most college students appreciate the flexibility?

Remember the girl with the 97? She will also be revising obsessively until 11:59 P.M. and will also start the rest of her homework after that. It's just human nature. If a policy is bad for students at both ends of the continuum, it's probably just bad.

December—Finals and Family

CHAPTER FOURTEEN

Yes, Exam Period Is Pretty Much as You Remember It.

For parents, December is very confusing. When our generation was in college, the month was spent studying for exams. Today's students spend the days between Thanksgiving and Winter Break preoccupied with: wellness! There are so many activities sprinkled throughout exam period that there's hardly any time to study! There are therapy dogs, meditation sessions, midnight study breaks, and caffeine everywhere you turn, 24/7. (Obviously therapy dogs and meditation sessions are necessary to counteract all the caffeine.) The pressure to keep up with all the wellness is really intense. You are simply too old to understand. I certainly am!

Occasionally, they have to take an actual exam. You would likely more or less recognize this ritual, except today's students take exams on computers. Confusingly, they often use an app called Blue Book, which is neither blue nor a book. (I better fact-check the blue part, but it's definitely not a book.) *Anyhoo*, it's your standard lecture hall full of young people trying to convince their professor that they have learned something during the semester, whether or not they have. And despite the rumors, there is no amount of caffeine or "cognitive enhancers" that can compensate for a semester of not learning anything. So exam period goes best for students who have been doing the work all semester, with or without the wellness activities.

Some things never change!

From my perspective, sitting in a quiet lecture hall taking an exam sounds relaxing, even meditative. It's come up that no one wants to meet me: That is, on the list of peers and professionals that university students look forward to meeting, the counseling center psychiatrist is just below *roommate from hell.*

That's at baseline. In December, it's even more so. On top of the requisite exams, papers, and wellness activities there's packing and travel planning, various performances and exhibits, holiday parties, and the occasional snowball fight. So no one is coming in for an appointment unless it's urgent. (Actually, there's a small number of students who are preparing for study abroad, and an even smaller number who graduate at the end of the fall term. These students usually just need to discuss a treatment plan. Phew.)

But mostly, there are various hair-graying scenarios that don't make it into medical textbooks. A student who missed the first day of class because he didn't feel like going and proceeded to miss every day of class for the entire semester. A student on a chemistry scholarship who is failing chemistry and hasn't told his parents. A student who had a panic attack and proceeded to stay in bed for three weeks. A student who took a drug at a concert and was subsequently hospitalized for psychosis. A student who hasn't replied to emails from her thesis advisor for a month. A student who has been disrupting an entire dorm since Thanksgiving. A student who partook in too many coffee breaks and not enough yoga breaks and had a panic attack. Lots of students like that. A student whose mind went blank during an exam. Lots of students like that. A student requesting an emergency evaluation for ADHD. Lots of students like that. Various laptop malfunctions resulting in no sleep and missed deadlines. Calls from other departments about all the above. Yikes, yikes, and more yikes.

None of these problems require rocket science, or even an fMRI. Most are some combination of poor self-care, poor planning, and poor communication, and have straightforward solutions involving improvements in each of these areas.

Oh, and usually quite a bit of paperwork.

■ ■ ■

One morning, I meet a rather purposeful young woman who is interested in increasing the dose of one of her medications before her final exams. Much to her annoyance, I do an assessment to see if I agree with her. She would prefer that I just do what she asks because she's busy, but she's in my office, not a coffee shop.

I immediately notice that she is on four prescription medications, which is a lot, especially for someone who . . . well, as far as I can tell, there is nothing wrong with her except for the fact that she is taking four prescription medications.

Well, there is one more thing. She has a *diagnosis*. This diagnosis didn't exist when I was in medical school but was quite common for a while. The girl believes there is something wrong with her because she has this diagnosis. And she has been to lots of doctors, who have given her lots of prescriptions.

Here's the problem. If you go to a doctor for just about anything, you get a diagnosis. Otherwise, the clinic can't bill and therefore won't be paid. So there's been a proliferation of diagnoses. This is a pretty obvious side effect, but there's another: If you give a person a diagnosis, they are likely to believe there is something wrong with them. This is a very serious side effect. Believing you are not well can make you live like a person who is unwell, which reinforces the belief, especially if you are constantly explaining how unwell you are. CBT, remember? Although in this case, the opposite.

And here's another problem. For the most part, doctors are quite reluctant to advise a patient to stop taking a medication prescribed by another doctor. But they are quite comfortable prescribing a new medication, even if the primary purpose of the prescription is addressing side effects caused by another medication.

This is what happened to the girl in my office. She had an illness that is quite common in teenagers, which often has a rather slow recovery, and left her somewhat weak. She lived in an achievement-obsessed community, so of course she couldn't cut back on her activities and take her time getting better. Good grief no! She might not get into Yale! So, her parents and doctors agreed she needed prescription medication to improve her energy, and her doctor prescribed *medication A*. They also agreed she probably needed more doctors, so she was referred to several specialists. The first consultant thought she was basically okay but could use more sleep—*medication A* was keeping her up—and gave her *medication B* to help her sleep. But then, she was having difficulty getting up in the morning, so . . . by the time she met me, she was taking two activating medications in the morning and two sedating medications in the evening. She believed she needed all these medications to function, and she had been taking them for over a year. Even though there was nothing wrong with her in the first place, apart from normal convalescence.

But she had a *diagnosis*, so she was asking me to increase her dose of *medication A*.

Which I didn't do.

I suggested that instead, we decrease her dose of one of the sedating medications. And over a period of several weeks, we decreased the sedating medications, which allowed us to decrease the activating medications . . . and so on . . . until she wasn't taking any prescription medications at all . . . and she was fine. Better than before, in fact, because she was saving lots of time and money on trips to the pharmacy.

For a few years while this diagnostic trend was raging, I had three or four patients like this every year. Patients who got better simply by stopping medications that they had been instructed to take. For a diagnosis that didn't exist when I was in med school. I shouldn't have had a single case like this in my career, and I've had well over a dozen, maybe more. My record was seven medications. That's seven prescription medications, all just chasing each other's side effects.

Thankfully, the trend has apparently abated, because I haven't had a patient like this in a few years. A diagnosis that didn't exist when I was in med school . . . might just not exist.

Need help now?

It's the family, not the college. It doesn't matter where they go to college—it matters what they do when they get there. I've seen students waste four years at BU, and I've seen students squeeze every last morsel out of their experience. I'm convinced this is true everywhere. What sets them up for adult life is their *relationship with you*, not where they get their degree. Relationships with teenagers are delicate—don't screw yours up by pushing them to improve their record to impress a slightly more selective college. It's not worth it.

CHAPTER FIFTEEN

Academic Pressure + Family Pressure = Pressure Cooker

The student in my office is pre-med. That's not a mental health problem, but that's what we're talking about. I love talking to pre-meds, because it reminds me of all the useful things I learned in med school. For example, I had an old-school professor who used to walk around saying, "A diet that works is cancer until proven otherwise." Can you imagine anyone saying that now? Those were the days! You definitely could not say that now! And I just did!

In med school I also learned that people in poverty are disproportionately impacted by every health problem that exists, but mostly our society doesn't do anything about it, and there is very little you can do as an individual to move the needle.

And at the fancy med school I went to, you also learn how to say U-rology and Neu-rology in such a way that no one could ever be confused as to which specialty you are referring to. This is super helpful, and you will definitely never forget it.

Also, you learn that child abuse is way more common than you would think, but you quickly forget it, along with everyone else except pediatricians, because this is way too depressing to think about.

Anyhoo, this particular student's parents have told her she has to go to med school, and she's from a culture in which if your parents say you have to go to med school . . . you just go to med school. This is almost impossible for Westerners to understand: There are many cultures in which children actually do what their parents say. This took quite a while for me to get my head around. But for her, the idea of not going to med school is about as feasible as walking through a wall.

If she doesn't go to med school, her parents won't be able to brag about her, which is obviously extremely important. I think to myself that she can get the last laugh by going into psychiatry. (Her parents will forever be stuck at cocktail parties explaining why their promising daughter went into psychiatry, instead of something self-important like neurology, I mean something important like neurology.)

Med school isn't her passion but she's fine with it, but there is one problem. She's worried about getting in. She just met with her pre-med advisor, whose primary job seems to be making students like her anxious. (I guess worrying is an important part of the process.) Her grades are good, but he's advising her to work in a lab and maybe do more volunteering. She's concerned about taking on anything more, because she already has a part-time job to cover college expenses, and barely has enough time to spend with her friends and get adequate rest. She seems reasonable to me. In fact, she seems like the kind of person who would make a good doctor.

I know exactly what is going on. Her pre-med advisor has determined that she is not stressed out enough. Her advisor knows that you need to be stressed out to learn well, so she has to be more stressed out so she can learn better and therefore be a better doctor. Everyone knows that. Actually, kindergarten teachers disagree. They have the completely misguided belief that students can only learn effectively if they're calm and relaxed. But what do they know? They're kindergarten teachers, not neuroscientists. All they have to do is teach people how to read.

Except kindergarten teachers have neuroscience research on their side. And research shows that to learn something as complex as reading, it is much better to be happy and relaxed. And research is not opinion.

So I guess this pre-med advisor thinks everyone wants a doctor who is stressed out and hasn't learned anything. Huh, that doesn't sound right either. Maybe he wants her to practice being busy and stressed out in order to be prepared for med school, when she will be doubly busy and stressed out, and for being a doctor . . . No, no one would ever become a doctor if they knew it was more stressful than med school.

You may have heard that there is a problem with physician burnout. In fact, I recently read about a study that concluded four out of five doctors would like to retire in the next month. I think that was the outcome; sometimes I don't get the details exactly right. Anyway, I think physician burnout might begin with . . . stressed out pre-meds. If they can't have balanced lives as undergrads, when are they supposed to start?

What do I know about being pre-med? Oh yeah, I was one. But I wasn't stressed out—at least not much of the time—and I had time for friends, and I played a sport, and I more or less got enough sleep. I mostly enjoyed my time as a pre-med student, and I now mostly enjoy my time as a doctor. And I simply can't believe this is a coincidence.

But the biggest irony of stressed-out pre-meds is . . . there are not enough doctors. One way to have more doctors would be . . . to have more med students, or maybe even more med schools. I think this is a good idea, but it must not be, because otherwise someone other than me would have thought of it.

Where I live, there technically are enough doctors, but they mostly don't see patients. They are too busy *improving* things to have time to *do* things. It's like with teachers. Idealistic young people become teachers because they want to help kids. But then they get a job in a school, where most of the helping actually happens, and discover that it's a lot of work. And they decide that if things were run just a little bit better, the hard work of teaching would be a little bit easier . . . for other people. So they get more degrees and then get fancy job titles where they . . . don't have to interact with children at all. So they're making things better for children by making things better for teachers! Except there aren't enough teachers, because they're all too busy getting more graduate degrees or working in an office somewhere, improving teaching. It's pretty complicated, but that's the basic idea.

That's more or less how it works with doctors. The usual career path is to train for a decade or so to become a physician, then discover that being a physician is really demanding, then decide that your time might be better spent doing research or improving health care in some way. So many doctors are busy researching and improving patient care that there is no one to take care of patients.

Now, every other person in my town is a doctor, so if you're on a soccer field and have a heart attack, you'll probably be fine. But if you try to schedule an appointment . . . forget it!

It reminds me of the time I had palpitations. Pounding palpitations that felt like the sort of thing I should probably go to the emergency room for, because I knew it wasn't a panic attack. But I was at my daughter's haircut, and you can't just leave daughters at haircuts because you think you might be dying.

But you also probably shouldn't do *nothing*, so I make an urgent appointment with my primary care doctor. She makes me wear a device with a fancy name that begins with a Z, because you definitely can't see a cardiologist until you wear a device that begins with a Z for two weeks.

I guess I should explain why the device has a name that begins with a Z. It means it is a brand-new product from a company with a large marketing budget. Marketing departments these days are compensated based on the Scrabble billing system. The higher the Scrabble score of the product name, the more they can bill. This is why so many new drugs and medical devices have long names that contain several Zs or Qs. I have no idea how they handle double word score; I obviously didn't go to the School of Management, I mean Questrom. Huh, is BU using the Scrabble billing system?

I wear this thing that begins with a Z for two weeks, or maybe it falls off after five days. I figure that's enough, so I turn it back in for interpretation to see if I'm still alive.

And I'll have to go in to talk to a cardiologist about it . . . when? There are no appointments available, ever, but between three kids and a job I don't have time anyway. So, I do what you do in my town. Which is to say, I ask my neighbor. Every other person in my town is a doctor, which means some of them happen to be famous cardiologists.

My neighbor looks at the results of my Z-test. He tells me I'm normal and there's nothing to worry about. (Technically, he told me my *heart* is normal, which is not the same as saying my whole self is normal, but that's what you hear when it comes from a famous cardiologist.)

I think we can all agree that it's a good thing he made me feel better, because otherwise we'd all have to . . . redefine the criteria for diagnosing an anxiety disorder.

This is how we survive the health care crisis in my town.

What on earth does anybody else do?

Depending on how old you are, you may be familiar with one of a number of TV shows based in a medical setting. There's *M*A*S*H, St. Elsewhere, Doogie Howser, M.D., Chicago Hope, ER, Scrubs,* or *Grey's Anatomy.* There are others, but you probably didn't watch them. Anyway, the medical environment provided rich material for the drama of human interaction, along with some high-stakes decisions and various existential crises. Good stuff!

You may have noticed that no one is writing any medical dramas anymore. *Grey's Anatomy* is probably still producing new episodes, but that's the exception that proves the rule because an AI took over the writing a few years ago. Don't believe me? Go ahead and watch the show. *Anyhoo,* no one is writing human dramas set in hospitals anymore for the simple reason that . . . there is no longer any human interaction in most medical settings.

And the reason for that . . . is Epic. Over the past twenty years, Epic has been slowly but surely taking over all of health care, and most people have never even heard of it. You see, Epic, the health care software that is dehumanizing the health care experience for patients, is also dehumanizing the experience for their health care providers. Most people just think their doctor is burned out or maybe doesn't have any social skills. But most health care providers now spend about 97 percent of their time wrestling with Epic, so they don't have time to talk to you. And that doesn't make good TV.

But Epic is here to stay because it is the only software up to the task of fighting your insurance company. So I guess we're stuck with it, at least until insurance companies decide to spend your money on your health care, instead of fighting with your doctor. In fact, pretty soon there's going to be no health care at all. It's just going to be hospital bots fighting to get paid, and insurance bots fighting to avoid paying. Wall Street and Washington won't even notice, so you're on your own, people.

Maybe my lovely pre-med's parents want her to go to med school so she can take care of them. Good thinking! And maybe the pre-med advisor is right. Maybe she should get busy being stressed out, so she can write an op-ed about burnout in ten years while her parents brag about her at cocktail parties. I better pretend I don't enjoy my job, so she doesn't get any subversive ideas about work-life balance. Better beat it out of her in college, before it's too late. If she is looking for human interaction in medicine, she can watch reruns of *ER*.

▪ ▪ ▪

My pre-med student isn't the only one whose parents had big dreams for her. I know of a mom who was angry when her daughter didn't get into Northwestern—angry at the daughter, not Northwestern! And an entire family that was in a state of collapse because the older son didn't get into Cornell. (Seriously? He ended up in Boston instead of the middle of nowhere, with the same school colors, and a better hockey team to boot. I'd say he dodged a bullet!) These people really need to read chapter seven. Young people need their parents' approval like they need oxygen, so reactions like this to arbitrary disappointments are a sucker punch to their mental health.

One student like this had a difficult relationship with his father. The student was a constant source of disappointment to his father because . . . he didn't like *hockey*. This student easily had an IQ of 150 yet somehow spent much of his adolescence fighting with his father about whether he had to keep playing his father's sport.

Mitzi never lets me call parents like these. I'm pretty sure she deletes their emergency contact information to be on the safe side.

They say love the kid you have, not the one you wish you had. This is good advice, not least because there's a good chance that the kid you have is *better.*

▪ ▪ ▪

One of the fun things about hanging around a university is the opportunity to meet smart people, including quite a few who are much smarter than I am.

I am about as smart as the average pre-med student, which has to be true if you think about probability for a second. I might occasionally *wow* you with my ability to multiply just about any number by thirty, or to remember the exact street address of a considerable number of pharmacies. Or I might underwhelm you by, hypothetically, forgetting to renew my medical license and allowing it to lapse. Well, that's a long story, and I asked if I could get fired for that, but the powers that be told me not to get any ideas.

Anyway, I was smart enough to go to a residency in psychiatry and learn quite a lot of useless information. However, I was not smart enough to remember most of it, which is lucky for just about anyone who has met me since then. Regardless, all this talking to smart people has made me quite good at guessing an individual's IQ. It's quite easy, if you pay attention to things like the complexity of an individual's speech, or the type of humor they enjoy, or what their major is.

Here's how it goes. If a patient is smarter than me, I consider their IQ to be about one standard deviation above mine, and figure they could easily be a cardiologist or an engineer. If I think they have a standard deviation on the typical cardiologist or engineer, then they could probably be an astronomer. Here's how to tell if someone is as smart as an astronomer: You just ask them how many universes there are, and if they can speak on this topic for several minutes while keeping a straight face, they probably have a stratospheric IQ.

This brings me to a funny story about BU. There is an astronomy elective that apparently fulfills a requirement for lots of students, because a considerable number end up in this class. Based on the number of students crying in my office, this is one of the hardest courses at BU. And when a certain kind of student tells me they are planning to take this elective, I tell them to stop everything and call their advisor *immediately*, because I know how it's going to go. Badly. I don't think the astronomy department is mean; maybe they just forget that most people have IQs closer to earth.

Guessing an individual's IQ is a little trickier if the student is in the humanities, because some people who think they're really smart are just really opinionated. The humanities don't have a natural scale of difficulty like the STEM fields, so you have to develop your own system. My own scale goes from George W. Bush to Winston Churchill, which accounts for just about anyone you might meet at a university. This is a broader scale than the pre-med to astronomy scale, probably in both directions. I mean seriously, would you want George W. Bush to be your mother's cancer surgeon?

Why do I spend all this time trying to understand how smart someone is? Does it matter above a certain point? I think it does. Because for the most part, a person whose IQ advantage over mine is measured in standard deviations . . . is often quite lonely. In fact, about every other year I meet someone for whom I think being too smart is the greatest source of their unhappiness.

Here's what it's like to be closer to the Winston Churchill end of the scale. You spend your entire life feeling like you are stuck in a traffic jam, with everything moving frustratingly slowly. Meanwhile, everyone else is honking and screaming at you . . . for speeding. I think it's lonely and frustrating. Not to mention terrifying, because you know that some of the people who control the nuclear codes weren't even smart enough to go to med school. I think if you're that smart, the world is lonely, frustratingly slow, and terrifying.

I love meeting people like this. I can barely keep up, of course, but I enjoy trying. I play it cool by nodding seriously or asking open-ended questions. That's kind of my thing. Anyway, when someone like this asks me what their problem is, I simply tell them. I draw an IQ curve, showing them where I think they are relative to random distribution, and discuss this in the context of their difficulty relating to people, which is usually what's causing their unhappiness. I don't think I've insulted anyone with this line of reasoning. In fact, it's rather validating and leads to productive discussions about how to relate to the rest of humanity. It's common to talk about intelligence as if more is always better, but I think, like extra height, it makes life harder after a certain point. A really tall person can occasionally commiserate with their friends about how annoying it can be to be so tall, but a person as smart as Churchill . . . mostly can't.

If you have been reading this passage and think I have been talking about you, please send me a message! Anything will do: postcard, smoke signal, morse code, whatever—just not telepathy because that would go over my head. I would like to hear from you.

Because here's the thing. In this work, sometimes a patient takes a little part of me when they move on. It's okay; it just happens sometimes, like with starfish on the beach: If you pull off a leg it leaves a scar, but also a space for new growth. Psychiatrists are impacted by our patients, sometimes a little, and sometimes a great deal. So I would appreciate a postcard.

And I guess where I am going with this starfish thing is . . . I don't think AIs can do that yet. I better go ahead and renew my medical license.

Need help now?

Play the long game. If you are arguing with your teenager, ask yourself if the position you are taking is more important than your relationship with your child. If it's not, drop it. Let them control as many decisions as possible. They want to dye their hair blue? Fine. (You don't have to pay for it!) They're room is a mess? Live with it. If it's about health and safety, hold your ground. No, they can't have unfettered access to the car.

There are gray areas, such as how much to insist on dinner with relatives. Grandparents live several hours away, and you only see them a few times a year? Sounds like a pretty high priority to me. What if they live down the road, and you see them every week? Maybe your teenager can occasionally skip it. Every scenario is different, but if the thing you're arguing about might not matter in five years, try to drop it. The relationship is paramount.

PART II

Spring Term—Advanced Topics

January—Required Reading

CHAPTER SIXTEEN

Isn't Mental Health More Than Just Adulting? What Else Do I Need to Know? The Big Three.

During my hospital years, I was responsible for teaching medical students. They were always smart and eager to learn but often didn't have much background in mental health. I wanted them to learn something they could carry with them—not so they could perform better on a test, but so they could understand humans. So I spent a lot of time talking with them about the Big Three.

In all clinical medicine, and certainly all of psychiatry, some people fare better, regardless of diagnosis. Some people bounce back, and others don't. This is driven by a million differences in resilience, emotional reactivity, frustration-tolerance, and the ability to seek help effectively, among other things. This isn't easy to comprehend, and it's difficult to teach, but it's also definitely there, and it's extremely important.

The biggest determinants of lifelong well-being happen before age five. Optimal human development requires a secure and loving early childhood environment. This is easier to study in other species. In rat pups, optimal development is determined by how many times your rat mom licks you. I'm not kidding! More licks equal a less anxious rat pup, and a better prognosis. This is actual science done by actual PhD psychologists! It is useful information, because it means fewer rats will need SSRIs.

Humans are a little more complicated than rats, and it's a little harder to isolate variables, but we know for sure that some things are very, very bad, especially before age five.

Child abuse, domestic violence, or a parent with an addiction. The Big Three. Each creates an unsafe and unstable early childhood environment, which is very bad for human development. For the purposes of this book, I am using the general term "child abuse" to include all its forms, such as physical abuse, verbal or emotional abuse, intimate abuse, and neglect. This is because I am primarily talking about downstream consequences of abuse, which are more or less indistinguishable. Child exploitation is a gray area. It's not always abuse but quite often is. It's a slippery slope. The easiest thing to do, just like with gymnastics, is to stay far away.

If you consider early childhood the runway of life, it's better to take off from a major airport, in a commercial jet. Flying has its risks, for sure, but commercial aviation usually gets you there.

Starting life with one or more of the Big Three is like taking off from an aircraft carrier. It's possible, but, boy, is it dicey. On average, if an individual has one or more of the Big Three, they have a narrow trajectory for a happy and successful life, and numerous ways in which things can go very wrong. And whatever challenges a person faces along the way will be worse if they have also endured the Big Three.

You have probably noticed that this book doesn't prioritize exploring diagnosis, and here's why. If a ship is sinking, it's important to understand the cause—that's diagnosis. But if a ship is sinking, it's even more important to understand how deep the water is—that's the Big Three.

Of course there are exceptions. You probably know of some prominent individuals who are survivors of the Big Three. Humans are capable of remarkable persistence and resilience. We can even launch a plane from an aircraft carrier in the middle of the ocean.

Okay, I didn't have much time with the med students, so I really had to keep it focused. They had a lot of stuff they had to remember from their other rotations. Well, obviously all they learned in pediatrics was the importance of child abuse. (Huh, that sounds familiar. That child abuse thing must be really important.)

You are not a busy med student, and I believe I can give you a basic framework to understand most of mental health in the next five to ten minutes: development and trauma.

Human development is a complex process that happens over decades; trauma is bad stuff that happens along the way, which can interfere with development. Trauma under age five is particularly bad for development because this is when young humans are learning the basics of emotional regulation and developing a blueprint for future relationships. These developmental tasks are critical for psychological well-being in humans.

It's currently more popular to talk about *neuroscience*. You could say events under age five are important because the brain is wiring rapidly during those years. If that's how you prefer to talk about it, feel free. Psychological development is brain wiring, and brain wiring is psychological development. Just ask any neurologist, and they will tell you they are right, I mean they will tell you I am right.

Trauma at any age can be harmful, but in general the older and more psychologically well-adjusted an individual is, the more trauma they can withstand. Many adults have careers that expose them to considerable trauma, and they can manage this with the right training, supports, and self-care. They can even thrive. But childhood trauma can have a significant psychological aftermath, particularly if it is prolonged and occurs at an early age. If you would like to understand this more, I encourage you to take an upper-level psychology class on trauma. Or if you prefer, you could take a class on Shakespeare and learn just as much and have more fun in the process.

Anyway, you can understand psychopathology pretty well if you learn the basics of development and trauma and then superimpose the various things that can go wrong, such as the diagnoses with the long checklists that you have probably read about but don't really help you understand humans.

There's one more thing you have to understand. Poverty. They mentioned it in med school, but mostly in the sense of things you can't control, so everyone mostly forgot. (Not like the Neu-rology vs. U-rology thing—everyone remembers that really well.)

Poverty is one of the most important variables in mental health, and everyone in the field knows it. You can't address mental health without addressing poverty, but I am mostly not going to talk about it, even though it's a much bigger issue on college campuses than most people assume. I could fill a book with an explanation of why poverty is important to mental health outcomes, but lots of people have written books like that, and those books are mostly ignored. The simplest thing to do is obviously to pretend poverty doesn't exist.

It's what everyone else does, after all.

If you would like to understand the link between poverty and mental health, I encourage you to take an advanced sociology class. If you don't have time for that, you could read one of several wonderful novels by Charles Dickens. That wouldn't save you much time, so maybe just take the class. But to save you the trouble, I'm going to spend the next paragraph summarizing the available research to bring you up to speed.

It's obvious.

That about covers it, while at the same time setting a new record for the world's shortest paragraph. It perfectly sums up what I would like you to understand about the link between poverty and mental health. And if I can't convince you with that paragraph, I frankly don't think I can convince you with an entire book, so we'll leave it at that.

So, from now on, we're just going to agree to ignore poverty like everyone else, even though we secretly know it's probably the most important determinant. Sound like a plan?

To put this all together, imagine a person is a flower. Flowers come in many varieties, but they all share certain characteristics. They all start from a seed. In the right circumstances, a seed will germinate and start to grow. A young seedling is very vulnerable to just about anything—conditions that are too wet or too dry, lack of nutrients, or simply being trampled or crowded out. The more established the plant is, the more it can withstand. Diseases can occur along the way. Early in a plant's life a disease might kill it or inhibit it from blooming. Later on, poor conditions might just reduce the number of blooms. A mature flowering plant will go on blooming and blooming even if you pick the flowers.

My job is to assess the flower that walks into my office. I don't get to see how the plant grew; I have to guess by evaluating the flower. The developmental history helps a clinician understand the level of risk and develop a treatment plan. Clinicians have to look at the flower and work their way backward to understand its growth and development. Mental health professionals are quite good at this.

This illustrates the importance of the early childhood environment. If a seed grows in nourishing soil with adequate sunshine, it will develop into a strong plant, which can then tolerate quite a bit of adversity. A seedling that is just hanging on in marginal soil doesn't have a lot of room for error.

Curiously, plants that are raised in greenhouses are often quite weak, though they grow rapidly and appear healthy. In the real world, they fade quickly. Growing in conditions that are a little too perfect makes plants weak. Flowers need a dose of adversity to be robust.

I would like to make another obvious point. A seed is going to grow into the flower it's meant to be. You can't change it. The flower can be weak or strong; it can be frail or robust. These outcomes are heavily impacted by environmental factors during development. But you can't change what *kind* of flower it is going to be. If you try, you can only harm it. You can't make it taller by pulling it up from the tip—that will just pull it up from the roots and kill it. You can't change a daisy into a rose, or vice versa. This will also damage or kill it. You can't make it shorter or skinnier, and you can't make it like the cello, never mind math or tennis.

The flower is going to be the kind of flower it is meant to be; that's a biological imperative. You can provide the optimal environment for it to grow well, or damage it. You can't change it. So just enjoy it. Even if it's a thistle. A thistle can be marvelous if you allow it to bloom.

Anyway, my med students certainly didn't have time to learn all that important stuff about flowers, so they just got the Big Three. It's not a perfect framework, but it's catchy and easy to understand, and it's not bad if you only have a one-month psychiatry rotation, which is all most doctors get to prepare them for a career of dealing with humans.

And it's not just mental health. Pick the social issue you are most concerned about, and the Big Three lurk in the background. Violence, incarceration, addiction, bullying, homelessness, teen pregnancy, police brutality, truancy, gangs, social instability—you name it, you will find the Big Three.

But wait, there's more. Want to see how the Big Three affect world events? Pick your favorite dictator or autocrat or infamous committer of war crimes. I challenge you to take a deep dive into their early childhood. More often than not, you will find one or more of the Big Three.

I developed this catchphrase to help med students learn, but I also use it as a shortcut for myself, to help me decide how much to worry about someone, especially if I'm in a hurry. If I'm worrying about a patient at home, my husband will ask if they have any of the Big Three. If I realize the answer is no, I will most likely be able to sleep.

▪ ▪ ▪

All that thinking about poverty is turning me into a communist. And the problems with health care are turning me into a socialist. But the blue state prescribing rules are turning me into a libertarian. So you can see that mental health is actually not political, and I have multiple personality disorder. But in a twist, you might not have foreseen, my field changes all the names of psychiatric diagnoses every few years to keep me on my toes . . . kind of like the tissues in my office. It's not called multiple personality disorder anymore, it's called . . . you are going to have to look that one up because I'm not responsible for teaching you everything. Because I sort of forget.

You see, my field publishes a diagnostic manual to keep things from getting too out of hand. It's the source of the symptom checklist you have to memorize if you want to convince your doctor that you have ADHD. The geniuses who make up the diagnostic criteria revise them every few years, as though the *content* of the lists is the problem, not the lists themselves. If you think of people as lists of symptoms, you're never going to understand mental health, but this is precisely the kind of thinking my field has been encouraging.

Anyway, the experts have to keep updating everything, so everyone knows psychiatry is real science. You know it's real science, because the people in charge all have numerous abbreviations after their names, and sit in endless meetings for months at a time. But there's a shortage of psychiatrists, so maybe it would be better if there were fewer people in meetings and more people seeing patients.

On second thought, maybe the people I'm thinking of should stick to meetings. The rest of us can stick to ignoring them.

Another reason my field has to update the diagnostic manual every few years is to make mental health seem complicated. Because otherwise everyone would figure out that to be well-adjusted most people just need loving families, supportive communities, and reasonable self-care. Plus, human nature completely changes every five years or so. That's why no one finds Shakespeare relatable anymore!

Need help now?

Whatever it takes, come home in a good mood. Take a walk, have a snack, or meditate before you walk in the door—whatever works for you. If you've had a bad day at work, don't expect an interaction with a teenager to improve your mood. I know, when they were little that bright smile could wipe away a stressful day in an instant. But that was then and this is now, and your teenager isn't going to do that. Putting you in a good mood isn't their job. Their job is to figure out how to be an adult, and to a very large extent they are going to follow your example.

CHAPTER SEVENTEEN

Why Modern Life Exacerbates Things (Early Humans Probably Had Better Mental Health).

Given the large number of contemporary teenagers who have grown up in totally optimal environments, the trauma framework isn't always the most useful in my office. If you ask me about my job at a cocktail party and I sense that you're game for a little more than advice on student housing, I'm likely to discuss mental health in an evolutionary context.

Much of what I do has to do with the disconnect between what nature intended and how we live now. I enjoy thinking about early humans, because it helps me understand the circumstances that evolution equipped us to handle. I happen to think that early humans had excellent mental health. This is not sentimentality or any particular ideology. I just think early humans had excellent mental health because . . . *otherwise they would not have survived.* If a group of humans had high numbers of adults with significant psychological problems that rendered them unable to work hard or collaborate effectively . . . they wouldn't have lasted long. So I think evolution equipped us for optimal psychological functioning in very specific circumstances, which resembled something like this.

Early humans probably lived in bands of a few dozen, maybe up to a couple of hundred. It was probably easy to remember everyone's name and face. Various ages lived in close quarters. Most everyone was probably outdoors most of the time. Healthy people did several hours of physical labor every day. People ate foods that were mostly unprocessed and consumed very few psychoactive substances. Children of all ages were probably given as much responsibility as they were capable of, which gave them a sense of agency. There was a considerable amount of caregiving, since small children and pregnant women had to survive for humanity to continue.

In the evenings, there was a campfire, for light, and to keep animals and insects away. People probably gathered around the fire to eat and socialize. And after a couple of hours, they went to sleep, because there was nothing else to do. Now, this is all my opinion, based on some general reading on the subject, as well as some guessing, and common sense. But I think it's good enough for this exercise.

I'm going to take this a little further. We are fully entering conjecture, but this is part of how I understand mental health. It was probably uncommon to meet strangers, especially for children. You have likely noticed that many children are naturally suspicious of strangers, which was highly adaptive for most of human history. Better to stay with your own group. They probably grew out of it on their own timeline, just like contemporary children.

I think early humans had very little privacy. This is an obvious point, if you have ever gone camping. But it's an important one, because I also think abuse was pretty rare among early humans. Why do I think this? Remember that humans have never been very good at surviving on their own, so remaining in good standing in a group was very important. Even a very strong individual could easily be extruded if several group members built a case and banded against him. So I think abuse was rare among early humans.

While our group of early humans was hanging around the campfire in the evening, there was probably singing. Yes, I think there has probably always been singing, for the simple reason that . . . it exists, it's relaxing, and it's a good way to get children to sleep.

And hanging around our group of early humans and their fire and their singing, there was someone else . . . a dog. Probably several. Providing company, playing with the children, alerting the group to danger, and chasing away rodents. Even then, the dogs probably didn't catch many rodents—sorry, guys!

Evolution didn't give dogs good hunting skills; it gave them awesome empathic attunement. (Empathic attunement primarily resides in the limbic system, not the cerebral cortex. Dogs have superior empathic attunement, despite having significantly smaller brains than humans. Human evolution favored a large cortex.) The dogs fed by humans survived better and had more puppies. That's how evolution works. So dogs developed nonverbal communication skills that are good enough to become a seeing eye dog or read a teenager, but the rodents are mostly safe.

Now, when I think about mental health problems that are common today, I often find myself thinking about how closely an individual's life resembles this model. What is their activity level? How much time do they spend outdoors? How much do they sleep? How much responsibility do they have in their community?

You can quickly see that a university is filled with people whose lives have very little resemblance to what nature intended. Scores of young people spend hours on end indoors in a library, under artificial lights. Caffeine is consumed in quantities, not to mention other psychoactive substances. An hour a day of exercise is the exception, not the rule. There are not many opportunities to take care of others.

People who exercise too little and consume too much caffeine are prone to anxiety disorders and sleep problems. Isolation leads to depression. Spending time around exclusively young people, as opposed to all ages, leads to lack of perspective, which can contribute to anxiety and depression. Drugs and alcohol are bad for the brain, and can cause mood and anxiety disorders, or even psychosis. Sleep deprivation is rampant and makes everything worse.

Plenty of people adjust fine to these conditions. Modern life isn't all bad. In fact, it's relatively good. But good self-care is no longer the default. It's something you have to consciously practice every day. Most people, with a little attention to their self-care, can function quite well in modern life. People can train themselves to go to bed earlier, minimize caffeine, prioritize social interaction, contribute to their community, and be more active. Kind of like living at your mom's house.

But for some people, modern life really doesn't work. Take ADHD. It's probably always existed, because the traits were fairly helpful for much of human history. For example, a high energy adult with a somewhat distractible style might have been effective at noticing intruders or prey or even keeping track of children. People with ADHD were probably well-suited to learning in an apprenticeship model, in which they were busy and active and had a lot of responsibility. What people with ADHD are not well-suited to . . . is higher education.

It's not just that living with ADHD makes college harder; there's compound interest. For example, if you're chronically struggling in your courses because of undiagnosed ADHD, you might feel bad about yourself, which might lead to depression. Now you have depression and ADHD, which is even worse. This scenario often leads to drug use, which again adds layers of variables. Everything in mental health can pile up like that.

Take anxiety. Remember our young child who was suspicious of unfamiliar adults, but was eventually going to grow out of it? That child was fine in our model of early humans. But now that child has to start kindergarten at age five, whether he's ready or not. Age five is the rule, so off he goes. Children are flexible, so most just get used to it. But for a few children, this is a disaster. They develop the idea that something is wrong with them because they can't get comfortable like everyone else. They have trouble making friends because they are anxious and don't feel like playing. They can't learn effectively, because anxiety impedes learning. And they develop the idea that they are the problem, as opposed to an inflexible system that requires all children to be on the same developmental timetable. This can lead to depression.

I also happen to think that anxiety has gotten worse, but not for the reasons printed in the newspapers. Anxiety is calibrated in a developmental context, and that context has changed. Take dogs for a second. Humans learned to live with dogs—living with them is not instinctual. As a result, it is quite common for small children to be afraid of dogs. As recently as when I was a child, this was handled with gentle teasing and a communal assumption that children would get over it, which we did. In the process, children learned that anxiety is sometimes an inaccurate assessment of risk and can easily be overcome with exposure and practice. (Sounds a lot like CBT, no?)

These days, if a child is afraid of dogs, adults shield them from any exposure. Parents call ahead and request that Fido be hidden away before a playdate. Dogs are banned from school drop-off and playgrounds. This is well-intentioned, but it results in children growing up believing their anxiety is an infallible predictor of risk, and that the world is truly as dangerous as they imagine. So their anxiety gets worse, instead of better. Protecting children from their emotions often backfires.

Modern life vexes us in other ways. Most people live in large cities, where we have to constantly interact with strangers. Nothing about evolution equipped us for that. Plenty of people adapt fine, but cities present a significant challenge for people with a tendency toward social anxiety or paranoia. It's honestly a miracle we can live in cities at all.

And electricity. Boy, has that been a disaster for perfectionism and sleep. You used to have to stop working at the end of the day because . . . you just had to. But with the electric light, you can stay up long past a reasonable bedtime, or even all night.

I talk about how I'm always encouraging students to take a look at their life and try to make it more closely resemble early human life in some way. How I often joke that contemporary humans have all the health and behavioral problems of animals in captivity. And how I'm always telling students that they are not the problem; society's demand for conformity is the problem.

There are excellent treatments available for a lot of these problems. And I prescribe them. But for the most part, I don't see my patients as having illnesses. I see them as humans, evolved to live in one set of conditions, but living in very different circumstances.

Of course there are some genetic illnesses that have probably always existed, but I happen to think most of them are also exacerbated by modern life. My list of reasons is long, but a quick summary would be: too much time indoors, too little physical activity, too much interaction with strangers, too little sense of community, too many chemicals, and too little sleep.

I tell stories of students I have met. Students who develop panic attacks because of inactivity, students who become depressed because they're studying philosophy instead of a breadmaking, students who wind up in the emergency room with panic attacks caused by various chemicals, students who want to spend more time with their fathers but don't know how to say so, students who don't eat enough in the name of fashion, and students who can't/won't/don't get enough sleep.

A few years ago, I was telling stories like this at a backyard party in my neighborhood. Various friends and family were present, enjoying a fire pit, with children and dogs playing in the periphery, and music in the background. (Huh. This is sounding a lot like our model of early humans. It simply can't be a coincidence that so many people enjoy gatherings like this.)

Anyway, I guess I ran out of stories, or maybe I needed some water, and eventually I stopped talking. I had been rambling, and sort of forgot people were listening to me. Honestly, I had no idea if anyone was interested at all. Oh well, I enjoy this topic, and it felt good to get some of it off my chest.

"You should write a book."

Come again?

This was about the last thing I was expecting. I was ready for questions, or polite interest, or a change of subject, or really . . . just about anything else.

I'm stunned, and somewhat flattered. But I can't write a book. I have nothing to say . . . Well, it's not true that I have nothing to say, but it's true that I *think* I have nothing to say, and no one would find it interesting, and no one cares about mental health anyway, and . . . I have an awful lot of carpool to drive.

Need help now?

A comment about teenagers and phones. If you are considering getting your teenager a cell phone, there's an issue to consider that doesn't get enough attention. *They steal chargers*. Boy, is this a problem. They lose their own charger, so they borrow yours, then promptly lose it. Rinse and repeat. There is no number of chargers that you can stash away to prevent this problem—they will just keep taking them. Their backpack is basically a black hole. Consider having an electrician hardwire your charger into the wall so it's there when you need it.

There's a less expensive solution, though. I simply label my charger with a short sentence in large letters. It works like a charm. That sentence? *My mom is awesome!*

February—Girl Talk

CHAPTER EIGHTEEN

I'm Not an Angry Feminist, but Women Really Do Bear the Consequences of Sex Unevenly, and This Has Mental Health Consequences.

By February, Spring is well underway. Not spring, Spring. In Boston, *spring* begins approximately one week before graduation, but most colleges insist on calling the second semester of the academic year *Spring*. I don't really know why; perhaps it's to trick kids into moving to Boston from California. Or really anywhere with more pleasant weather, which is just about everywhere. I guess it's working, because Boston is a popular destination for students.

February is punctuated by snow days and Valentine's Day, the twin nemeses of working moms. Snow days equal no childcare and housebound kids; Valentine's Day equals nonstop sugar highs and endless art projects involving glue and glitter. Pick your poison. Feminists are always talking about boycotting Valentine's Day, and maybe they're on to something. I guess they know they can't control the weather.

A graduate student has an appointment. As much as I love talking to teenagers all day, there is a certain relief that comes when I see someone over the age of twenty-five on my schedule. Adult conversation.

This student has a history of depression and is doing well on an SSRI. That is, her *depression* is in remission, but she is not exactly doing well. She is having significant sexual side effects. She wants to discuss going off her SSRI, because she reads the newspaper, and there are stories about SSRI-induced sexual side effects every day. But she's also afraid of her depression coming back, which is a very reasonable thing to fear because she is in grad school and can't afford a semester-long setback.

I do a little more asking. She's also taking an oral contraceptive pill, also called an OCP or birth control pill, or simply, the pill.

Huh.

By the way, I should tell you a couple other things you learn in med school. You learn that all women over fifty should be taking hormone replacement therapy, because it's going to make them live longer and not break bones and not have heart attacks . . . except they're going to reverse that one five years later . . . and reverse it again ten years after that. Oops.

But the most important thing you learn in med school is that women are too stupid to keep themselves from getting pregnant.

Boy, do you learn this. And you believe it, because it's med school, and you've gotten into med school by being a dutiful student. You believe it even though you are a woman yourself, and you have met plenty of women who have somehow kept themselves from becoming pregnant.

So, doctors believe in the pill, because it is "the best" birth control, and women certainly shouldn't be trusted to manage their own bodies.

Um.

Except the pill has one small problem. Well, maybe more than one problem, but one teensy problem that I am going to talk about because it relates to this lovely student sitting in my office.

The pill causes sexual side effects in as many as half of women who take it, ranging from decreased libido to total anorgasmia. Anorgasmia, which means inability to orgasm. Oops—isn't the point of the pill for women to be able to be equal participants in their sex lives?

The patient in my office is a sophisticated adult who has been reading the newspaper, so she's pretty sure her sexual problems are caused by her SSRI. But now I know she's also taking an OCP, and her OCP is equally likely to be the culprit. The pill causes sexual side effects in rates that are through the roof, and no one ever talks about it.

Except *I* do.

"Let's talk about sexual function in women," I begin. I tell her that sexual function has neurologic and endocrine inputs. The neurologic input comes from the brain, and is disrupted by things like stress, lack of sleep, and SSRIs. The endocrine inputs come from, mostly, testosterone. Yup, testosterone, even in women. The ovaries produce a little bit of testosterone as part of the normal process that makes estrogen. Some of it gets out, and contributes to a number of processes, including sexual response.

OCPs work by shutting down the ovaries, so endogenous testosterone production stops. We could easily replace testosterone in the pill, but we don't. Why? Because we care about whether women get pregnant, not whether they have orgasms.

I sometimes think about the counterfactual, in which scientists invent a birth control option for men that causes sexual dysfunction in up to half of them. A better feminist might find this depressing, but I find it funny. Actually, hilarious. So hilarious that whenever I'm in a bad mood and need cheering up, I think of a marketing department tasked with promoting a birth control option for men that causes sexual dysfunction. Makes me laugh every time.

So, I present the options to her. We could taper her SSRI, and risk her falling into a depression that might put her another semester behind in school. We could switch to a different antidepressant, which would take weeks and may or may not work, and may or may not solve her problem. Or she could use a different birth control method for a while and see if that helps.

She chooses the latter. She hates the pill, anyway. It's causing bloating, and if she takes it more than an hour late, she experiences mood swings and spotting. She honestly seems sort of relieved that someone has suggested stopping it.

It works. She's grateful. And she's somehow avoiding getting pregnant. Do I push her on what she's using for birth control? That's what I've been taught to do, because, you know, the thing about women and avoiding getting pregnant. But I don't. She's an adult, and I'm pretty sure she knows her body better than I do.

▪ ▪ ▪

Next there's a quiet girl in my office who I sense needs a therapy referral to one of my colleagues.

I should pause for a minute and talk about some of the different roles in my department. I am a psychiatrist, which means I completed medical school and a four-year residency training program. A psychiatrist is necessary for the few college students who may need medication or who may have medical problems underlying their mental health symptoms. Psychiatrists are trained in psychotherapy as well, but there are only a few of us for a whole university. We usually refer therapy cases to colleagues, who have various degrees in social work, psychology, and education. Only a tiny fraction of the students who come to our clinic require a psychiatrist.

The girl in my office has low self-esteem and is not sure what she wants from life. She's not even sure why she scheduled the appointment. She's unhappy but not depressed.

For the sake of thoroughness, I'm reviewing her medical history and glancing at her chart. She hasn't had a mental health visit before, but she's been in to see primary care quite a few times.

I'm scrolling through her visit history and see a Plan B visit. Plan B is also called emergency contraception. (Back when I met her, a doctor's visit was required to get the morning-after pill, so there was a record.) I scroll down a little more, another Plan B visit. Huh. A third. A fourth.

Four Plan B visits in nine months. This is a red flag.

I ask her about it. Is she in a relationship? Does she want more information on birth control options? Is she safe?

Well, she's not in a relationship, and she doesn't really want to discuss birth control options, because she doesn't really want to be having sex... But there's this guy she hangs out with, and every once in a while he pressures her for sex, and she wants his friendship, and she doesn't want to disappoint him, so she always tells him it's the last time, and she doesn't want to risk pregnancy.

So she uses Plan B every couple of months, feels miserable for a couple of days, and moves on.

Feeling miserable for a couple days after Plan B is pretty common.

The guy doesn't seem to have any side effects at all.

Is this what the sexual revolution wanted? I don't think so. But it's one of the consequences. Young women with low self-esteem who don't want to have sex, pressured by someone they know into sex they don't want, who used to be able to at least hold up the I-don't-want-to-get-pregnant card, and now can't even rely on that. They are out there and I have met some of them.

Today, anyone can just go to a pharmacy and buy Plan B. No questions asked. And this is progress, I guess, because having to go to a doctor is patronizing. But if you have to go to a doctor maybe, just maybe, you meet someone like me who notices your plight and tries to help.

One other thing you learn in med school is to be patronizing. Very, very patronizing. You're taught every day that you are smarter and know more than everyone else. Otherwise, you would quit, because med school is also very, very hard, in every possible way. I have spent most of my career trying to beat the patronizing out of myself, because it mostly doesn't help people.

Except when it does.

So I don't refer her to someone else for therapy. Instead, I suggest we schedule another appointment.

I think about my daughter and cringe.

▪ ▪ ▪

I'm on triage again and get a heads-up that a girl is coming in with a panic attack. Bread and butter.

A panic attack is sort of like a smoke detector going off. Red alert! It could mean a fire, but most often not. Usually, you're trying to determine what set it off at the same time you are trying to stop the ringing. And frequently it's a dead battery. But sometimes it's a fire.

So I'm getting ready with deep breathing exercises and progressive muscle relaxation and trying to understand the few words that are coming out of her mouth. She's not making sense; she needs to breathe a little more.

She had a fight with a male friend. Hard to understand if that's important. Still hard to understand anything. More breathing. She's late. Don't worry, whatever it is can wait. Take your time.

She's talking about going to CVS to go get a test. Oh, she's that kind of *late*.

I call primary care and speak with one of the nurses I know well. "I have a young woman in my office who came in with a panic attack, but really she needs a pregnancy test." "Oh," the nurse replies. Bread and butter. "And she doesn't want to sit in the waiting room because she's still in the middle of a panic attack."

My colleague is in my office before I can hang up the phone.

The girl is back in my office in less than ten minutes. Pregnancy test negative, panic attack resolved.

Every human female from ages fifteen through fifty lives every day with the possibility of being pregnant. Depending on the person and where they are in the arc of their life, that possibility represents a risk, a chance, a hope, a longing, or a regret; but it's always there. And if it happens, it's either a crisis or a miracle. There's really nothing in between. Every day.

That stuff can really mess a person up.

▪ ▪ ▪

I'm assessing a young woman with depression. She's referring to something that happened about a year ago. She's clearly avoiding it. I ask what was going on last year. "I . . ." she trails off. She thinks for a while, then starts again: "I had an abortion."

She's embarrassed, but not quite. She's embarrassed *about* being embarrassed. "I just didn't know . . . well, I'm pro-choice and everything, and it was definitely the right decision . . . but . . . I just didn't realize how *hard* it would be."

I know. I have worked with countless women during and after their pregnancies. I have known women who have lost pregnancies at every stage, as well as women who have, due to mental illness, given up a child for adoption either voluntarily or by court order. I have worked with women who have lost a child or been forced to leave a child behind in another country.

And all these women who experienced this loss after even a few weeks of pregnancy carry it with them for the rest of their lives. If you ask, they can tell you how old their child would be, and what they might be doing. This is not good or bad, it just is. The minute a pregnancy begins, the mother's brain starts rewiring. Reproduction is a biological imperative, and sixty-five million years of mammalian evolution have programmed her to preserve the pregnancy at any cost. Individual free will is no match for biological imperatives.

So yeah, she didn't realize how hard it would be. Because that's not how we talk about abortion. We don't talk about it like it's a terrible crisis that requires support. We talk about it like you have to be in one camp or the other, and you're probably evil if you're in the other camp. This conversation isn't helping young people.

Of course, a woman should be able to choose whether to have an abortion. But that's like saying she should be able to choose whether to amputate her left arm. What a terrible situation! I guess if you're right-handed, maybe it's not such a big deal. But still, it's your *arm*. Imagine it has a condition that would change your life forever, or affect your health in some important way, and you have to decide whether to keep it. This is a terrible decision! But everyone is saying it's not! It's just like having a mole removed! But you have sixty-five million years of evolution telling you to preserve it, because it's your left arm.

Do people regret having abortions? Sure, they do. Some of the most pro-life people came to their passion after having an abortion themselves. But they don't really want to talk about how hard it was, because that would mean acknowledging they had an abortion. Even though it's evil. But it wasn't evil when they had one, just necessary. But now they've seen the light and know it's evil. At least for other people.

The fact that neither side is allowed to talk about how difficult abortion is makes it harder for the actual people who are in crisis.

I once had a miscarriage. It was sad, but I moved on because that's what you do. But you can't move on unless you get to be sad. Grief is part of the process. It wasn't the same as having a mole removed. It was a pregnancy that wasn't meant to be. And I'm fine with that.

But I also know how old the child would be. Adult, actually.

So I listen to the girl in my office. Her roommate took her to the procedure, but otherwise her friends were clueless. They all knew about her pregnancy, and they were pro-choice and supported her. But here, I'm using "supported" in the sense of saying "I support you," as opposed to actually listening. They acted like she had a mole removed. Procedure's over, so it's over, right?

No, it's not over. She'll remember it for the rest of her life.

But that's not bad. It just is.

Abortion doesn't cause mental health problems. But I'm pretty sure the way we fight about it does.

You may have noticed that most of my patients are female. This is true for almost every mental health provider in the country. Officially, no one knows why. There's lots of hand wringing on the topic. The people sitting in meetings create working groups and issue proclamations about how pressing this issue is. Then they shrug and say it's probably too complicated to fully understand. And yet, I've never met a female clinician who is surprised or confused by this fact.

CHAPTER NINETEEN

Birth Control Has Consequences, Too, Which Is Confusing, Since It's Supposed to Be About Prevention . . .

The next student in my office engages in pretty risky sexual behavior. She's having sex with a different person every weekend, which is not very common, despite what pop culture may lead you to believe. She tells me it's fun, but it sounds like she's trying to convince herself. She honestly seems rather hollow.

I had this mentor in my residency training program who was interested in women's sexual health: She studied the female orgasm. She used actual scientific research . . . the kind with neural pathways and hormones and data and publications. And for applying scientific rigor to the female sexual response, she was . . . mostly ridiculed and marginalized. But she *persisted*. I guess she cared more about whether women had satisfying sex lives than about whether her mostly male colleagues valued her research. Anyway, she had this totally insane idea that a woman's satisfaction with her sex life might be related to . . . whether she is having orgasms.

So, I asked the very sexually active but seemingly dissatisfied young woman in my office whether she was having orgasms. Her answer?

I don't know.

I don't know!!! She is obviously not having orgasms. How exactly did we get here? You have probably already guessed it—she was on the pill. Her doctor and her parents must have known she was too stupid to avoid getting pregnant. In her case, she was *so* stupid that they put her on birth control when she was fifteen, four years before she became sexually active. She has never known her natural sexual response. And she is having sex often. And she has never had an orgasm. And her male partners seem to be just fine.

Well, this got me curious. Was she the only one? Unlikely—that's simple probability. I find appropriate times to ask about it. In my job it's often appropriate and relevant to ask about sexual health, and it is occasionally appropriate to follow up with a neutral question about whether the patient is having a healthy sexual response. I am especially likely to ask if I know the individual in my office has been taking the pill since her mid-teens, which is quite common. Over the course of my career, considering the number of patients I see per year, and how common this issue is . . . I see it over and over and over again . . . and over and over . . . and over and over again . . . feeling good yet?

Anyone who missed that should just read on and pick the book up again in a few years. Don't explain it—they'll blush.

Young women starting birth control before they are familiar with their body's sexual response and therefore being unaware that they are having sexual side effects, is an important issue that no one is talking about. My evidence? When I mention this at a cocktail party, the reply I typically get is some version of . . . *Huh, that reminds me of my college roommate, who couldn't have an orgasm. It made her boyfriend feel bad.* (I warned you, I'm a pretty weird cocktail party guest. Please keep in mind that I'm only telling stories I consider appropriate for publication.)

Between my clinical experience at the office and informal chats at cocktail parties, I think this is rather common. Now, in the case of mental health, my sample is skewed, because people who come to see me are generally unhappy. However, in the case of sexual health, it seems probable that my sample is more random and is therefore representative of the population at large. I think there are a lot of young women like this out there.

This is not a life-or-death issue for the young woman in my office, except *now* it might be if she makes the mistake of getting pregnant—depending on where she lives. (If she gets pregnant, I guess you would say that her birth control failed her twice.) But this is an important sexual health issue that should be spoken about. I'm writing, but *metaphor.*

The overall passage kind of works as a metaphor, too. Women quietly not having as good a deal as men but going along with it because they don't quite know what they're missing.

Are there completely legitimate reasons to prescribe birth control pills to fifteen-year-old girls? Of course! You have already encountered PMS. Then there's a whole range of concerns from acne to cramps, and of course contraception. But I think the prescription should come with a warning, particularly for girls who are not yet sexually active. Because they are likely to have sex eventually, and *surely* a healthy sex life is about more than avoiding pregnancy.

Need help now?

Don't take anything personally. Most of the time, their mood has nothing to do with you. It's going to change in fifteen minutes anyway.

CHAPTER TWENTY

Eating Disorders: How to Create or Prevent Them. Yup, Everyone Has a Role.

Another eating disorder. How do I know? Oh yeah, we haven't reviewed the criteria for diagnosing eating disorders. You have already learned that psychiatry publishes a diagnostic manual full of lists of criteria that mental health professionals are supposed to memorize, but that I find too boring to read.

Anyhoo, they change the criteria every few years, and even the names of the diagnoses, so the easiest way to diagnose an eating disorder is just to ask the patient how much Diet Mountain Dew they drink. If they give you a look of confusion and disgust, they probably don't have an eating disorder. If they answer, "I drink a two-liter bottle of Diet Mountain Dew every day," they probably have an eating disorder, most likely anorexia. It's practically pathognomonic. (I'm pretty sure eating disorders are the only reason Diet Mountain Dew comes in two-liter bottles; maybe even the only reason it's on the market.)

But I didn't even have to ask whether she drinks Diet Mountain Dew, because she came into my office carrying a bottle.

So I save a bunch of time on the diagnostic criteria, which I probably don't remember anyway, and skip ahead to asking about how and when it started. She had a happy childhood with lots of friends until her dad got a new job and moved the entire family when she was in sixth grade. *I'm stunned.* I have seen this movie before. Happy-go-lucky child moves to a new town in sixth grade, and morphs into a miserable teen with an eating disorder. I've seen this movie so many times that I've memorized the script.

It doesn't have to involve moving; any major life event at age twelve can have an outsized impact. This could include divorce, a death of a caregiver, immigration, or even a global pandemic.

By now, you are all experts in the Big Three, so you are probably surprised that I am discussing sixth grade. You are pretty sure that the most important stuff, whatever it is, happens by age five, and you're right. However, I am going to introduce another critical period of development, the early teenage years.

Everyone knows that kids start changing quickly somewhere around age twelve or thirteen. There are the obvious physical changes, as well as brain changes, which are associated with increasing capacity for complex thought and complex relationships, including a preoccupation with social hierarchies. A lot is written about these topics, and you can delve as deeply as you want. To vastly oversimplify, children up to about age twelve look primarily to their parents for social support, while teenagers look primarily to their peers. This should be easy to remember because it is obvious to anyone who has ever been a teenager or met a teenager. How an individual enters this transition is quite important. Are they well adjusted? Do they have lots of friends in their community? It's probably going to be an easy transition. Did they just move? Do they have any of the Big Three? Higher degree of difficulty.

Think about it another way: Imagine an adult human is a building. A building needs scaffolding until it can stand on its own. For children, the scaffolding is mostly their parents. For teenagers, it's their peers. The second scaffolding is not quite as good. You'd better hope that scaffolding is replaced carefully, and that the new scaffolding is strong enough to last. And you can't control this.

That's a common attitude, anyway. But there is a culture I am familiar with that is rather well-known for throwing a large party for each member of the community on their thirteenth birthday. So every individual, during the critical time when their scaffolding is being replaced, has a day in which everyone in their community celebrates them and tells them they are special. And based on what I know about development, and my own career in mental health, I think this is . . . a very good idea. Not coincidentally, this cultural group is also well-known for particularly strong community ties, high achievement, stable families, and low levels of criminality. Managing the transition to the teenage years is critical.

When I was twelve, my superpower was empathy. This doesn't make me unique. Now, empathy is a pretty good superpower to have if you are a mental health professional, but it's not a very good superpower to have in middle school. I was skilled at understanding a friend's point of view, but unfortunately not very skilled at knowing whether it mattered, which created some . . . confusion.

You see, all my friends were constantly mad at each other. They were always arguing about . . . I think they were arguing about which Duran Duran song was the best. Or maybe something else that seemed important at the time. Anyway, they were each so persuasive and I could never pick a side, so I was just sort of befuddled.

Except for one friend, the one whose mom was dying. She was never arguing about which Duran Duran song was better. She just didn't seem to care. She had *perspective*. And although I was twelve and didn't know about broken thumbs yet, I knew that a dying mom is more important than a Duran Duran song. This is to say that part of why middle school is hard is that almost no one has perspective. Because for a twelve-year-old, the price of perspective is quite high. So, if your teen or tween spends all their time arguing about Duran Duran songs, just be glad that they don't have perspective. And don't move to another town where they don't have anyone to argue with.

And don't worry about looking up Duran Duran—it doesn't exist. It's just a metaphor for things that are forgettable.

I am not a very good example, because I turned out rather boringly okay. But let me give you an example involving a famous family. Let's call them the thoroughbreds. You know them; they're even more famous than the Bushes and the Clintons. Sorry, we have to pause for Gen Z to look up those families . . . Everybody back? Anyway, the thoroughbreds are sort of a cult.

When the oldest one died recently, they changed an entire national anthem from *God Save the Queen* to *God Save the King*. They just did it, and everyone went along with it—right away! Imagine the commissions and working groups and congressional hearings this would have to go through in our country. You may recall that I live in a town that spent three years renaming a school.

Here's what you need to know about the thoroughbreds: There were two boys who had a lovely mother and a deadbeat dad. (This might be a confusing example because their mother rather famously had an eating disorder, and I don't know anything about her life at age twelve. So I'm going to digress and tell you that controlling relationships are also quite effective at causing eating disorders.)

Anyway, the lovely mother died in a tragic accident when the boys were twelve and fifteen. I'm using the word "accident" here in the sense of my gymnast and her life-changing "accident." No one knew precisely when it would happen, but in the overall arc of her gymnastics career, it was the logical conclusion to a series of ignored warnings. Or like ski accidents at Deer Valley, which . . . we've covered that; skiing there is practically asking for a serious injury. The lovely mother's accident was one of those slippery slopes: It's a slippery slope from harassing someone to driving them to serious mental health problems . . . to just killing them.

So these boys lost their mother and were left with just their deadbeat dad. Too strong? That's what you call it when a man ignores his wife and kids and gallivants around publicly with another woman. The boys were in a terrible situation. But they were not in the *same* situation. The fifteen-year-old had already switched to his teenager scaffolding. He had gotten through his early years thanks to his mom and already had a solid group of teenage friends. He was able to grieve and move on, relatively unscathed by his father's incompetence. But the twelve-year-old—he is more mustang than thoroughbred—was just left without any scaffolding at all. So the mustang did what mustangs do when they are lost and injured—he ran wild. And how did the thoroughbreds respond? The way thoroughbreds always respond: by hiding in the stable with blinders on.

You can see that while these two boys went through the same event literally, they didn't go through the same event *developmentally*, and it had a huge impact on the next decade of their lives. So, major life event at age twelve? Better make sure there are caregivers who are paying attention.

I make a few quick notes to myself, because I have to persuade my husband that we can't move while any of the children are in middle school. He naturally agrees, because he is extremely supportive. I don't mean supportive in the sense of saying, "I support you;" I mean it in the sense of taking my opinions seriously. He also agrees because he works in an industry that only exists in the Boston area, so it's a moot point. I can scratch that worry off my list, which is good, because if my list of worries gets any longer . . . we might have to change the diagnostic criteria for anxiety disorders.

Don't want to pick up the whole family and relocate, but still want your daughter to develop an eating disorder? I've got lots of ideas—I've honestly barely gotten started. You already know about modeling and ballet and gymnastics, the triumvirate. Then there's the old standby—the gold standard, really—private all girls' school, the more elite the better. (The *school* doesn't cause the eating disorders, of course, it's just a total *coincidence* that half the graduating class meets criteria every year.) Then there's high school girls' cross country; very effective, particularly if you are also interested in creating lifelong debilitating stress injuries. Don't forget controlling relationships—very effective, though not the most common in the age group I work with. And of course, doing any of the above in combination will increase your success rate.

All those things sound too expensive and time-consuming? Okay, you don't have to do any of them. Saying any of the following can do the trick: Are you sure you want more ice cream? Do you realize how many calories are in that smoothie? Don't you think that skirt is a little tight? Why doesn't that dress fit anymore? Think you can fit back into it by graduation?

Any of these questions will be particularly effective coming from a father.

But don't worry, moms have a role, too. All you have to do is constantly obsess about your size or shape, talk wistfully about dresses that no longer fit, or just generally send the message that appearance is more important to you than health or well-being. This seems to come naturally to many moms, so you probably won't have to work very hard at it.

How often do you have to make a comment like this to make sure it sticks? Possibly as little as once.

That's right. An individual with an eating disorder often has a very specific memory of what started it, commonly an offhand remark from a parent about weight or shape. The parent typically has no memory of making this comment. It is one of the themes in this book that your grown-up-looking children are hanging on your every word, and eating disorders are no different. A comment you have long since forgotten may have run through their head hundreds of times, with potentially profound consequences.

You need to move while your kids are in middle school, and now you are concerned about the implications? Don't worry about it. Seriously! Your kids will probably be fine, especially if they don't have any of the Big Three. Humans are adaptable, and most of the time people turn out okay. But to be on the safe side, give them lots of your ears and time and love or placebo.

Need help now?

Calibrate expectations appropriately. I'm planning a party this weekend. I'm buying champagne and inviting all my friends and colleagues, because I am celebrating something big. What's the occasion, an award or major milestone? No, much bigger. Earlier today, I overheard my teenage son say the following to his girlfriend: "My mom is usually right about stuff like that." *Wow!* This is a day to remember!

People, this is the appropriate reaction. Praise or acknowledgment from a teenager is not to be expected; it should be rejoiced. In general, neutral is about the best you can hope for, eye rolls and one-word answers are common, and insults and door-slams are within the norm.

They spend their days out in the world being mostly pleasant and appropriate, and they don't feel the need to put in the effort at home. They are not trying to hurt your feelings. Of course not! They aren't even aware that you *have* feelings!

March—Madness

CHAPTER TWENTY-ONE

Beware the Ides of March—Youth Sports

The student in my office was "committed" to go to a college to play his favorite sport. Well, he was committed, but it turns out the college, which was also my college, was not committed. And he made the mistake of being in a serious car accident during his junior year of high school.

When he awoke from a coma there was a letter from this college, which was also my college, telling him to get well soon. Right? Wrong. The letter was telling him that since he could no longer play his sport, they were no longer committed to him, because they needed someone to play the sport. Because the sport was more important than his humanity. (That's not what it said, but that's what it meant.)

That's right, this famous college, which was also my college, told a seventeen-year-old who had barely survived a serious accident and was now significantly disabled, that they no longer wanted him. Because they needed someone to play a sport.

So he did what any seventeen-year-old would do in this situation. He became depressed. Because this college, and this sport, were his dream. So now he's in my office because he is a student at BU because he wanted to be . . . right down the river from . . . oh no, he's going to think about this every day.

I used to love my college, but now I can barely acknowledge it.

My college broke my heart.

Another student. This one played tennis and loved it. He got pretty good too. Good enough that his mother had to get him a better coach, in a better club, where he didn't have friends, because if you're good at a sport . . . obviously you have to get even better. It's never enough, just like with beauty.

But now he didn't enjoy tennis much because his friends weren't there, so his mother got him another coach. Because maybe the coach was the problem and not the fact that he missed his friends. And he was improving—at tennis, anyway—because that's what kids do. So there kept being better and better coaches farther and farther away, until . . . there was no longer time for anything but tennis and driving to tennis.

So he quit. To spend time with his friends. Because he was a kid. His mom was furious, because he was really good at tennis, and if he kept going for just one more year, he could probably have gotten a scholarship so he could play in college and . . . continue to be miserable.

So here he is, in my office because he's depressed—depressed because he doesn't know how to do anything other than play tennis, and now he hates tennis.

Well, I don't completely blame his mom because you may recall that the parenting pandemic was raging and I guess she got caught up in it, because beliefs are quite contagious.

But I do blame her for not vaccinating herself, because even then there was a vaccine available, and it was cheap and readily available, and it's called . . . being reasonable.

And it doesn't have any side effects.

So anyway, now he hates his mom because she ruined his childhood, and she hates him because he quit tennis. And they might eventually make up and get over it. In fact, they probably will.

But you can't get your childhood back.

And *she* can't get his childhood back, either.

And another. Football this time. Lacrosse too, but mostly football. He had six concussions in three years, all under the age of eighteen. And now he's a college student, but that is not exactly how I would describe him. He's a body, walking around a college campus. He's definitely sad, and has a sense of loss, but I wouldn't call him depressed. He struggles in his classes, struggles with focus. He doesn't have ADHD exactly, but he sort of does. He's kind of numb, and quite lost. It's hard to make a diagnosis. He doesn't currently have a concussion, that I'm sure of. But I doubt he was like this before.

I can be confident that his concussion has resolved because that is what his neurologist said. Hopefully he saw a Neu-rologist and not a U-rologist, because that is a mistake you could easily make if you didn't go to my fancy med school. But in this case, it would also explain a lot, because he is not better.

I try to help him, but I don't think I do. Time helps him, a little. He has a therapist too, and occasionally we get together and commiserate for a while, feel sad, curse youth sports, and shrug.

I think about my children and cringe.

Everyone has gotten the message about kids and drugs. To keep kids off drugs, they have to do sports, and the more they do sports, the more they don't do drugs. I guess.

But sometimes the sports can be worse than drugs.

At least it's all worth it when they have a coveted spot on a college team.

Did you believe me just then? Hah—I was playing with you! Well, it's what I wish. But it's not what I see. What I see is that collegiate sports can be a nightmare for some of the young people who participate in them.

The girl in my office is talking about her sport. Her coach is a bully, and she's miserable. She hasn't mentioned the sport yet—sometimes students are a little uncertain about how confidentiality works—but I'm able to guess immediately. She's surprised, but it wasn't even difficult. Half her team has been to our office, and that's just this year. We've known about this coach for years. Think about that for a second. And year after year, students have gone up the chain in the athletic department with their concerns about this coach. Think about that for a second, too. Now, the coach eventually disappeared. But a quick back-of-the-envelope calculation, multiplying half the team by several years equals . . . a whole lot of mental health problems caused by a single bully coach. And this is a sport with no career path for women. So it exists in college only for the experience itself, which in the case of this team, was ruined by a bully coach.

Why don't they just quit? Reasonable question. Some do, but they're not the ones who find themselves in our office. They are the ones with options, and life always goes better for people like that. Students on athletic scholarships have fewer options. Leaving their sport may mean leaving the university, including all their friends and a half-completed degree. This is not an easy decision for a twenty-year-old. They may be better off sticking it out with a bully coach for another season or two, or at least they may think they will be.

The next student has an injury and, based on the contraption she's using to wheel herself around campus, I'd say it's pretty bad. She's overwhelmed. Getting around campus is a struggle. She needs more rest than usual for recovery, and physical therapy takes up about two hours most days. This is leaving her very little time for homework, because . . . her coach is requiring her to continue attending all the team's regular practices. She has spoken with her coach and tried to compromise on a reduced schedule, so she can do her homework. The athletic department is backing up the coach, even though last I checked this is a university, and this is definitely a sport no one cares about. (I keep the last bit to myself, because obviously the student in my office cares about it!) I have long since begun to wonder if college sports are beyond redemption, but she apparently hasn't.

With an exhausted expression, she asks, "If the NCAA cares about student-athletes, why don't they have a hotline that students in my situation can call?"

Great question, and it leaves me speechless. It left me speechless at the moment, and it still does. What takes my breath away is the notion that some student-athletes out there still think the NCAA might care about them.

The student in my office has been depressed for over a year. Not just depressed—she has an eating disorder. She didn't do ballet, or any of the triumvirate, or go to private all girls' school. She didn't have any adverse events around age twelve and hasn't even been in a controlling relationship. Still, she has an eating disorder; so how did that happen?

Well, she did grow up in a world with entire industries devoted to making women feel bad about themselves in the name of profit. That's a good start, but usually not enough by itself.

Luckily, a couple of years ago her coach figured out how to cause more eating disorders! You see, this student has played her sport for years. She has always loved her sport, which made her feel strong and powerful, and generally positive about her body. Her sport was also my sport, and eating disorders used to be quite rare in this sport. But her coach has figured out a way to make eating disorders common! You simply weigh the athletes constantly, then rank them and proceed to obsess about the ranking! This works quite well if you have a group of competitive people, such as a group of college athletes. So within a few months, half the team had an eating disorder. (This would be a good time to mention that eating disorders are highly contagious and also supercompetitive. Once eating disorders are established on a team, they are difficult to eradicate.)

The student in my office was able to win this particular competition by not eating. Unfortunately, this had side effects. She developed a recurrent injury, which wasn't healing. She became depressed due to being exhausted and malnourished. Her pain and frustration from the injury exacerbated her depression. (Mental health problems can really snowball.) By now she's been struggling for over a year. She doesn't need surgery, but she's in pain most of the time. Her coach is impatient. There's pressure to play through the pain. Her sport stopped being fun a long time ago. She can't quit; her identity is tied up in her sport, and she can't imagine her life without it, never mind the side issue of her scholarship. She loved her sport for years and can't believe it's come to this.

But today, she seems happy. I've never seen her like this. Is her injury better? What? Her injury is worse. Her doctor has told her she has to quit her sport. *She's delighted.*

Am I missing something? Yes—this is a new one for me. Since she has been medically dismissed from her sport, she gets to keep her scholarship and finish her degree. So her dilemma is solved for her, and she is no longer depressed. And she is no longer being weighed every day. And she is eating again. And she feels like her old self. Well, except for her injury, but that will get better now that she is eating.

I could have filled this entire book with depressing stories about college sports. They're broken beyond repair. And I'm only talking about the mental health fallout from college sports, not the many other issues you are more familiar with from the general media. This saddens me because I loved sports, and they were an important part of my own development. But I've had to leave those memories behind, because college sports are broken.

Except when they're not. She's in my office. She has a broken thumb, something that requires her to see me a couple of times a semester, but she's fine. Or am I the one that needs to see her? She loves her sport. And she's strong, and more or less happy. Her sport helped her grow confident, which is how it's supposed to be. She reminds me of me. I want to tell her that, but I don't, of course. (Because of professional boundaries, but also because of the bewildered expression she'd make. I definitely don't remind her of herself, because I'm twice her age.) She's on an athletic scholarship and never would have afforded college without it. She is squeezing every possible morsel out of her four years.

So it's still possible.
But it's not what always happens.
Because sometimes there are side effects.

Need help now?

You know when your spouse is being unreasonable. Don't dogmatically agree with your partner or spouse in the name of presenting a unified front. This works for toddlers, but teenagers see right through it. If your spouse is being intransigent, nudge the conversation in a different direction, or politely suggest that you take it from here.

CHAPTER TWENTY-TWO

Is Everyone with Mood Swings Bipolar? No.

There's a mom in my office. Her son is in the hospital. He's manic, which is part of bipolar disorder. She wants to talk to me. She's a famous cardiologist, and she's dressed the way you do if you live in New York and you're famous.

I'm dressed like I have two kids under the age of three.

She asks if I can give her some studies on lithium—she wants to look at the original articles. I'm in semi-panic. Do I even really know what the seminal articles are? Could I find them? Could I interpret the graphs? Could I talk about the inclusion criteria or the drop-out rate? Definitely not.

It's not just me; it's a problem of my field. This is the era of evidence-based medicine, but the evidence in my field requires . . . a whole lot of interpretation. We mostly don't have studies that tell us the things we need to guide treatment, like which medicine is the best in a particular situation, or how long the patient should take it. These would be useful things to know.

We do have studies showing that one medication is better than another for four weeks, or at least maybe it is, until you think about side effects and then it's sort of a wash. We also have studies showing that certain medications are better than placebo in specific situations, or at least they separate from placebo statistically, or at least they do for a while.

This is not the kind of thinking that impresses a famous cardiologist, and certainly not coming from a woman with no fashion sense who hasn't slept and isn't from New York.

So here I am talking to her, feeling inferior. I suggest, "The residents can pull some articles for you." This is something we can agree on: asking the residents to do the busywork. And it gives me a moment to think.

Then I do what I always do when I'm not sure what to say—I ask questions. It's always appropriate to gather more history, so this is never questioned. She starts telling me about raising her son and all she's been through with him, and also about her career, years of infertility, and how lost she feels.

I realize I have something to offer her. I tell her that her son is safe while he is in the hospital, so she should rest. He will need her more when he is discharged. I had this conversation hundreds of times during my hospital years. Families are always relieved to be given permission to go home when their loved one is hospitalized, and it also happens to be true.

I also tell her not to worry about the research. It's impossible to digest, and the studies are mostly not generalizable. But more to the point, I tell her that in this situation, she is the *mom*, not the doctor. Her role is to watch movies and laugh with him, and do his laundry, and feed him, and tell him to go to bed on time.

That is what he needs from her right now.

And this is what she needs from me right now.

▪ ▪ ▪

Another manic patient. Mania is the defining clinical feature of bipolar disorder. It most commonly occurs in March, for reasons that elude us, but definitely predate basketball. (I should clarify that this is true in the northern hemisphere, where I work. I don't know which month has the highest prevalence of mania in New Zealand. I'll have to put this on my list of interesting questions that I will probably never have time to look up.)

I guess this would be a good time to tell you what mania is. It's more or less the opposite of depression, with elevated mood, increased energy, and other associated symptoms. What's bad about that? Most people with mania would also like to know. Being manic can feel good—like a natural high. Unfortunately, it doesn't last. It can spiral up into psychosis, or down into depression. Like many things, it is relatively easy to control in its mild forms, but more difficult to control in its more severe forms. So we try to treat it in its mild forms before it becomes more serious.

The student in my office was brought in by his roommates because he's been talking really fast and keeping them up all night. Sure enough, he's talking fast. I have to interrupt him frequently to keep the assessment on track; otherwise, we'd be here all day, and I have to stay on schedule so I can get to carpool on time. He meets many of the other criteria, too: decreased need for sleep, distractibility, grandiosity, laughing at my jokes . . . oh yeah, that last one is a particularly bad sign.

This has never happened to him before, so while I am assessing him, I am also teaching him about mania specifically and bipolar disorder in general, which isn't exactly easy when you can barely get a word in. I tell him it would be helpful if he would consider taking medication for a few days to bring him back down to earth a little. He acknowledges that something isn't quite right, but has concerns about medication, and asks if there are any alternatives. Happily, there is an alternative . . . stimulus restriction.

Stimulus restriction. It's just as boring as it sounds. Basically, it involves not doing anything exciting, turning the lights down in the evening, going to bed early, maintaining a basic routine, avoiding caffeine or other stimulants, and eating healthy food. That's it. It's basically like living at your mom's house, which you may have noticed is extremely boring for college students or people who are manic, and the young man in my office is both. But stimulus restriction can keep a patient like this out of the hospital.

In fact, stimulus restriction is one of the main reasons hospitalization is so useful for treating mania. You see, a locked psychiatric unit is about as boring as your mom's house. Well, it's boring unless a patient with mania has been admitted, in which case it is very exciting. In fact, the student in my office reminds me of an MIT student I took care of several years previously, who was admitted for mania and got better despite not wanting to take medication.

This is how it went. One morning, I arrived at the hospital and everyone in the staff meeting was talking about this MIT student who was manic and believed he could walk through walls. I should clarify that it was common to draw attention to patients who were considered *flight risks* because it presents a significant liability to the hospital if a patient just leaves, for obvious reasons. So he was considered a flight risk, because he was talking about walking through walls, but not in the sense of the Kool-Aid Man or Edwina the Dinosaur. He was talking about sort of oozing from one side of the wall to the other, which everyone thought was insane. And everyone agreed that he needed antipsychotic medication ASAP.

I had taken care of a number of MIT students at this point, because the hospital where I worked was nearby. Several would be admitted to our unit each semester, most often around exam period. Exam stress? Nope. Sleep deprivation, mostly. (*It's that important!*) I knew enough about MIT students to know that while they are occasionally insane, they are usually insanely smart. So I went to meet my new patient and ask him about walking through walls.

He was chatty and somewhat euphoric, both of which are part of the diagnostic criteria for mania, and also rather persuasive. He explained that most matter is just nothing, because matter is made of atoms, which are just protons and electrons that are miniscule, and nothing in between them, which is just nothing. So a human is mostly made of nothing, and the wall is also mostly made of nothing. In theory, if the atoms lined up just right, the mostly nothing of a human body could sort of ooze its way through the mostly nothing of the wall.

At this point I checked for my key in my pocket, so I don't have to rely on oozing through the wall to go home at the end of the day. Sure enough, I have my key, which means I'm the sane one in this conversation.

It reminds me of *A Beautiful Mind*, a movie that you probably haven't seen if you are under the age of forty but should. The theme of the movie is that mathematicians are generally more handsome than you would think. Sorry, that's not it. The theme is that it can be a slippery slope from genius to insanity, and it's not easy to tell where, or even whether, someone is on that slope, particularly if they are smarter than most people.

So with MIT students in particular, I have to be careful, because most of them are frankly smarter than me, and I am the one holding the key. Luckily for MIT students who are hoping to get discharged from the hospital anytime soon, I'm skilled at differentiating insane from insanely smart. (There are rules about how long someone can stay in the hospital, and under what circumstances, so they would eventually get discharged anyway. But they still probably feel lucky to have me as their doctor because I am obviously so charming and personable!)

I'm a little uncertain about this oozing through walls thing, so I will have to consult with someone smarter than me. And I happen to know an astronomer, and astronomers are total nerds, I mean insanely smart. Some astronomers are probably insane too, but this one isn't. He's insanely normal. (He's a little mean, though; he insists on starting every day by beating me at Wordle. Sigh.)

So I consult with the astronomer about the oozing through walls thing, and he shakes his head and explains that though it's extremely unlikely . . . it is theoretically possible. It seems that everything is mostly nothing. Well, this gives me some good ideas for handling the problem of plastics pollution, but at the moment it puts me in . . . a really bad situation. You see, if I explain to the nursing staff that the oozing thing truly does present a flight risk . . . they might take my key away from me . . . and then there would be two of us needing to ooze through the walls to get home at the end of the day.

I obviously can't tell everyone that he's basically right, but I do tell him. And I also tell him that I don't think he needs to take an antipsychotic, which he had reasonable concerns about. But I do think it would really help if he would get some sleep, and he agrees to take medication for that.

And after a few days of sleep and stimulus restriction he's ready to go back to MIT, so I let him out the door with my key.

Anyway, the student in my office doesn't need to go to the hospital. But since this is his first manic episode, neither of us knows how bad it could get. I generally prefer it when a patient accepts a prescription in this situation, though that's no guarantee that they would take the recommended medication. Stimulus restriction is hard for college students to pull off—it's frankly an overstimulating environment. That's kind of the point of college.

So we come up with a compromise that we can both live with.

He agrees to go home to his mom's house.

■ ■ ■

My door was open and a student wandered into my office. This used to happen in our old office layout. A student could occasionally wander in off the street and end up in my office. Or anyone, really, such as someone looking for the arena, which is a very, very huge fancy building just across the street. Or a student looking for the registrar, which is in the same building, but you have to go outside to get there. At least that's what I tell them. I have no idea where the registrar is, but it gives me enough time to shut my door. Phew.

But this student is looking for a psychiatrist, so he's wandered into the right place. He's running out of lithium and needs a prescription. I haven't done an assessment, and I don't have time in my schedule today. But lithium is not the sort of thing you want to run out of if you are on it. So I write him a prescription and schedule an appointment.

To schedule an appointment using our office software, you have to confirm the identity of the patient with their date of birth. This is one of my favorite parts of my job. Seriously! You wouldn't believe the observations I have made about birth dates, and birth years. When I first started at BU, most of the freshmen were born the year I graduated from high school. You notice that. Along the way, the birth years that predominate become the years of personal events, like the birth years of my nephews, and world events, like 9/11. You definitely notice that. Now, we're almost up to the birth years of my own children, and that's going to be super weird. And soon after that, we'll be up to 2014, which is the year that *1989* came out—wait, what?

Well, those are my observations on birth years, and time marching on. For the purpose of confirming his identity, I just need to know the month and date.

So, I'm scheduling an appointment, and I ask his birth date. This birthday will be easy for me to remember. I'll enter it every time I put his name in my schedule for the next four years, without checking. I'll remember it through ups and downs, watching him grow into himself, in spite of his illness. He graduated years ago, but I still remember his birthday and think about him most years on that day.

It's my birthday.

CHAPTER TWENTY-THREE
An Honest Discussion of Suicide Risk.

One morning, I arrived to find the office door locked. This doesn't happen very often, for obvious reasons involving getting children ready for school. However, we have meetings on Thursday mornings, so the doors remain locked until 10 A.M.

Many students have never heard of the internet and can't be bothered to check our schedule, so on any given Thursday a few lost students turn up while we are closed and stand outside looking confused. I usually say good morning and point out the very obvious sign where our clinic hours are posted.

On this particular morning, a student standing by the door caught my eye and said, "I'm suicidal," so instead of pointing out the office sign, I invite him into my office.

So now, instead of getting a cup of coffee and catching up with my colleagues, I'm doing a safety assessment on someone I've never met.

I wonder to myself if the student has already taken something or is carrying a weapon. Both are possible. In a hospital setting, an individual like this is searched before being evaluated. This increases safety but is also aversive, so it is not routine in an office like mine.

I get busy. A mental health crisis typically involves a stressful event, the individual's response to stress, and their recent baseline. I need to understand all of these variables. Frequently, talking about the precipitating event dysregulates the individual even more, so I need to avoid that, while still getting the relevant information. I need to understand something about this individual's level of functioning and social supports, as well as whether they have ever been in treatment. It would really help to know about the Big Three, but there isn't time for a full developmental history. Luckily, I know shortcuts.

My phone rings. A colleague saw me bring the student into my office and wants to know if I need any help. I reply that I'm fine, but I will be missing the staff meeting.

Of course, that's not quite true. Well, it's true that I'm missing the meeting, but it's not exactly true that I'm fine.

The truth is, this is where I'm meant to be.

■ ■ ■

Meghan is at my door. She's our case manager, because we've entered the twenty-first century and we have a real live case manager.

Technically, she's our second case manager. Our first case manager was . . . a little scary. I don't work during the summer, but most years a few new people join our department while I'm off. When I come back in the fall the new people don't always know what to make of me. Our first case manager didn't know if I was a serious professional or a mom held together by duct tape, and I made it difficult for her by generally appearing to be a mom held together by duct tape.

But the thing was, I had put a huge amount of effort into trying to make her job exist. Because we really needed a case manager. So I launched a relentless campaign. I brought it up in every staff meeting for five years, which gave me a certain reputation for persistence. And I may have sat on a secret university committee for a year and written a significant part of a huge document that ended up on the university president's desk. Because although I am seriously allergic to meetings, I do think people sometimes need to sit and discuss problems. Also, they asked me nicely, and said I would be home in time for dinner. But mostly, I did it because we needed a case manager.

Anyhoo, I probably shouldn't be talking about secret university committees, so forget I said anything. The report sat on the president's desk for several years and nothing happened . . . and now, suddenly, I have a case manager. And I secretly love President Brown, who has since retired, because he got me a case manager.

That's not the only reason I secretly love President Brown. I secretly love him because he once acknowledged me. He sent me an email to thank me for my work. Apparently, a student had bothered to tell him that I was helpful, maybe by suggesting leaving fifteen minutes earlier to get places on time or something. I'm not sure. But President Brown sent me an email to thank me. And he didn't have to. No one would have known if he didn't. Not even me.

And I have kept it, because that's what you do with nice letters from university presidents. It's right here in my drawer next to me. Or at least I think it is, but we had a pandemic and I spent a lot of time at home and now I've switched offices and I've lost track of it. But I still have it. Somewhere.

Our first case manager didn't know all this, and I looked like a mom held together with duct tape, so she treated me . . . professionally.

Which is to say, she was a little scary.

But Meghan is never scary. And Meghan doesn't look like anyone who was once mean to me, which is good, because she has to come by my office almost every day. You could never be afraid of Meghan. She is like a golden retriever or a perfect kindergarten teacher—honestly a great way to start the day. And now she's at my door, wanting to talk to me.

And this is great. I enjoy talking to Meghan. I tell her that when you're considering having children, no one ever tells you how much paperwork you're in for. After a dozen years of motherhood, I'm still buried in paperwork almost all the time. She should consider this, if she is thinking about starting a family. Also, we talk quite a bit about *The West Wing*, because she's watching it for the first time.

And I probably also talk about my youngest child and how I never have time for him, but at least I have never lost him anywhere, or at least not for long, but . . . well, there was that one time he fell out of his stroller and fractured his skull. When he was three months old.

But it was okay because children are resilient and the pediatricians were nice because pediatricians, while they know a whole lot about child abuse, also know about accidents. Except there was one person, a social worker who didn't know about accidents, who did accuse me of child abuse, which is more or less the worst thing you can do to a mother who is having one of the worst days of her life. Well, she didn't exactly accuse me, but I knew enough to know that was what she was there for. And she was mean.

Which is to say she was *professional*, instead of kind. But she could have treated me kindly because it was one of the worst days of my life, and because it was an accident.

And even if it wasn't an accident, she *still* could have treated me kindly because it *still* would have been one of the worst days of my life. Because I definitely care more about my son than she does. Sixty-five million years of mammalian evolution have made it that way.

Plus, he's insanely cute.

I didn't complain, because I was the one who had just been responsible for an infant falling on his head and I was probably totally exhausted, but I'm pretty sure she didn't understand her job. Protecting families means supporting families, not kicking them when they are down.

Despite this experience, I have never committed child abuse, at least not yet. But don't tell my kids because now they are teenagers and I don't want to give them the upper hand.

This social worker looked slightly like our first case manager, which is possibly why I found our first case manager a tiny bit . . . scary.

Meghan listens to me. Maybe no one has told her that I'm only kind of a doctor, so you only kind of have to listen to me. At least, she always looks like she is listening to me.

But there is one small problem with Meghan. One teeny, tiny, enormous problem. She never has good news! Not once, not one single time, has she dropped by my office first thing in the morning with good news. That's right, there's only two kinds of news with Meghan: bad news and terrible news.

Today, she has terrible news. A patient of mine attempted suicide over the weekend and is now in the hospital. There is no worse way to start your day. Actually, there is one slightly worse way . . . Come to think of it, news worse than a suicide *attempt* would probably come from someone higher up than Meghan.

I'm dumbfounded. "That's impossible," I react. This particular student wasn't on my radar as particularly high risk, and I am befuddled and flustered, which by now you probably assume doesn't happen very often. I pull myself together enough to think through her risk factors. None of the Big Three, no psychosis, not much substance use. Pretty bad case of the parenting pandemic, though. Huh. She's a senior. Would've thought the effects had worn off by now. A high degree of perfectionism, though. Huh.

Over the course of my career, I have spent hundreds of hours speaking with seriously suicidal people. The range spans from individuals having thoughts of suicide for the first time up to and including people who have made one or more serious suicide attempts. Because of my years of hospital experience, I have evaluated numerous people in the immediate aftermath of an attempt, or in the weeks following. In my experience, suicide attempts usually involve at least one of the following: insomnia and/or sleep deprivation; substance intoxication or withdrawal; psychosis or recent psychosis; poverty; recent trauma or loss; the Big Three; perfectionism.

It's worth staying with the last one, because it is extremely important in the population I work with, which is high-achieving young people. Perfectionism isn't just about eating disorders and anxiety. It is a huge contributor to many suicide attempts that I know of. Remember the girl with the 97? Imagine how poorly equipped she is to handle any of life's true disappointments. And think about the suicides you read about in the newspaper, where everyone is shocked because the young person had so much going for them. The story is often perfectionism, which is an extremely toxic side effect of the parenting pandemic.

In short, a suicide attempt is primarily driven by the individual's state of mind in the moment, as well as their immediate personal circumstances, usually combined with being alone and having access to something dangerous.

The most serious thoughts of despair are generally fleeting, and people usually change their minds. This is the entire basis of identifying suicidal people for support and treatment. It is typically a temporary state, like severe pain or nausea. I have talked to people at length about the process of their suicide attempt, including what method they chose, and why. Happily, humans are much more robust than most people think, so people frequently survive suicide attempts. Many even seek help themselves. Some describe a survival instinct that kicks in, triggered by pain or fear; others describe an ebbing of a tide, back to a point where things seem manageable again. So quite often, an individual seeks help during or immediately after their suicide attempt.

The difference between a suicide attempt and a suicide is a coin flip. In their moment of desperation, which may have lasted as little as fifteen minutes, what did the individual do? Did they take a bunch of pills? Depending on what they took, they're probably going to be okay if they get help fast enough. Self-injury? Same thing.

Talking to patients in the wake of a suicide attempt helps a mental health clinician understand how to help that person avoid getting to that point again and dig their way out if they do. It is not an exact science, but clinicians are good at this work, which is why engagement in mental health treatment is so protective. Most people can move on from serious suicidal thoughts and live a full life, just like most people can move on from severe pain or nausea.

But there is one kind of suicide attempt that I have never been able to ask someone about—a suicide attempt by firearm. Because that is not a coin flip. There is no serious discussion about suicide prevention without addressing access to firearms. We have no reason to think the mental state of someone who attempts suicide by firearm is different from the mental state of other suicidal people; the difference is access to a dangerous method. And clinicians are honestly powerless on this one.

Clinicians can, however, break the taboo about talking about suicide methods, and I think it's time. It's long been considered gauche or disrespectful to discuss the means by which a suicide death occurs. I think if there were more public understanding of common suicide methods, there would be more acceptance of simple safeguards, such as locked rooftops or gun cabinets.

The most intense drive for suicide can last as little as fifteen minutes. So, if a suicidal person goes to the top of a tall building, finds a locked door, and heads downstairs to find another building, the moment often passes. Or at least recedes enough to call for help. Numerous people have described this experience to me, and the existing data support this concept. Restricting access to means is a very effective component of suicide prevention, because intense suicidal ideation is a transient state. Like pain or nausea.

So lock up your guns. And if a suicide death occurs by firearm, say it. Don't accept the status quo.

No one wants a suicide. And the real tragedy is, this probably often includes the suicide victim. At least, it is quite likely that the victim only wanted to die for a very short time and could've moved on to have a full and happy life.

▪ ▪ ▪

A new student is in my office, so I'm taking a history. You have probably gathered by now that when I'm not trying to persuade people to sleep more, I'm mostly asking questions. So I guess my job could be done by an AI after all—huh, I haven't really been worrying about that, but maybe I should. Anyway, she attempted suicide last April—her senior spring of high school—so I ask what was going on around then.

She tells me that she tried to kill herself because she didn't get into Yale.

Yale?! Are you kidding? Someone attempted suicide because she didn't get into Yale? I mean bulldogs, seriously? All that drool, and those upper respiratory problems!

Wait, that's not where you thought I was going with that. Oh, you thought she was suicidal because someone told her she had to go to Yale . . . That would honestly make a lot more sense.

I'm still not getting it right? You're offended? Me too. I'm deeply offended that the parenting pandemic and the insanity around the college admissions process have created a culture in which it is possible for young people to believe that if they don't get into a certain college, their life is literally over.

When I am talking about the parenting pandemic, I am not just talking about burned-out eighteen-year-olds, though I meet lots of those. Where there are lots of stressed teenagers, a subset will have significant mental health problems. And where there are teenagers with significant mental health problems, a subset will become suicidal.

And I know of some deaths.

Actually, I believe there are a lot.

You see, I meet someone like this about every other year. Someone who attempted suicide during their senior spring of high school, after getting rejected by a specific college. In fact, I have a list of these colleges—the colleges I directly associate with one or more suicide attempts. I'm not trying to have this list; I just can't get it out of my head. I bet I'm not the only one. I bet many mental health professionals and some high school guidance counselors have lists like mine. And there's something funny about my list: It closely resembles another list you are probably familiar with. That's right—the rankings. You see, my list resembles that list so closely, it can't be a coincidence. A fun game would be to publish my list next to the more famous list (well, infamous now), and have everyone guess which is which. Something tells me Harvard wouldn't like this game much.

I think the issue of serious suicidal behavior surrounding college rejections is more common than you would like to believe. And literally no one is talking about this, let alone trying to collect data.

Oh, sorry, I'm not supposed to be talking about suicide so much, because it might be contagious. Except I don't believe that. Remember how much time I have spent talking to suicidal people? I have spent a significant chunk of my professional life over the past twenty years talking to seriously suicidal people, and I have never once caught it. I have caught Covid, influenza, Coxsackievirus, and various GI illnesses, and . . . are you following? But I have never once caught suicidal ideation.

Okay, it might be a tiny bit contagious, but to catch it you have to be susceptible, which in the case of suicide generally means spending a lot of the time wishing you were dead. So, if there is a suicide in a high school, you shouldn't talk about it because . . . so many high school students are walking around *wishing they were dead*?! Okay, people, if so many high school students wish they were dead, don't you think we need a plan a little more proactive than just not talking about suicide?

We are going to talk about it, because that's the only way to understand it. Think about heart attacks for a second. They're obviously very bad. But what if no one talked about them? What if we just treated heart attacks like mysterious events that can't be understood? Occasionally they are, but most heart attacks occur in the context of several risk factors that are well-defined, like high blood pressure. Now, high blood pressure is a completely boring condition that doesn't even have symptoms. You would be totally justified in ignoring it completely if it weren't connected to heart attacks. But a heart attack that occurs in the context of years of untreated high blood pressure isn't a mystery at all. In the same way, a suicide that occurs in a pressure-cooker high school in a community with hyperintense, high-achieving parents just isn't a mystery. It's a consequence of unaddressed risk factors.

There might not be any reason to care about high blood pressure if it weren't for heart attacks. But once you understand the connection, it seems crazy to ignore it.

Suicide works the same way. There are risk factors that are well-understood, but not by the general public. So we need to talk about it more.

It is my opinion that the parenting pandemic and the insanity accompanying college admissions contribute significantly to youth suicide. I believe this, because it is what I have seen. Cases like our would-be bulldog are the tip of the iceberg. I hear about even more suicide attempts that occur in the general milieu of a highly competitive high school experience. Students tell me about "suicide clusters" in their schools. These are often prestigious institutions with very good college placement data. I just consider them high schools where a lot of students have mental health problems. And for many of the students that I meet, their only real basis for a mental health problem is . . . that they went to one of these high schools.

Of course, high school students are generally older than twelve, and definitely older than five. So am I talking about an overall impact like the Big Three or important life events around age twelve? No. And does an adverse background predispose a student to worse outcomes in high school? You bet. In general, the students who are most impacted by a toxic high school culture were already struggling. *But the numbers are so big that some otherwise well-adjusted teenagers will die by suicide because of this environment.* Just like some people with untreated high blood pressure will die of heart attacks.

I think this toxically competitive culture around college is an important cause of the uptick in mental health problems and suicides in young people, but I don't have the data to prove it. Because no one is looking for it. Because no one knows it's there. This is a problem of research; it relies on human thinking. You only look for something if you think you might find it. So, poof! Cell phones cause suicide, and the college admissions process doesn't. That's what everyone is saying, so it must be true. Who am I to contradict the prevailing opinion? *I am a psychiatrist who has worked exclusively with college students for nearly two decades.*

Now, what if she had gotten into Yale. Would she be better off? Not really. If you don't believe me, call their counseling center. They're overwhelmed, too. This degree of preoccupation with perfectionism, and the lack of preparation for setbacks that goes with it, are poor preparation for adult life. When you turn the teenage years into a winner-take-all competition, it doesn't end well. Even for the winners.

Luckily, I have some helpful suggestions as to how the college admissions process could improve. (Actually, I have helpful suggestions on any number of topics—the world is going to be a much better place when I am in charge!) While college admissions are not my wheelhouse, I'm rather adjacent because college mental health is. And college admissions is a huge part of the adolescent experience for much of this country.

Elite colleges, are you ready for my ideas about improving the admissions process?

Make it random.

I think you should consider dropping your entire admissions process and accepting students at random. Just take every high school senior who expresses interest in attending your college and draw names out of a hat and *poof*—there's your freshman class. You could use a computer program if you prefer, but I would obviously just draw names because of my issues with technology.

Oh, I forgot about your academic standards. I have an easy fix for that. To enter the drawing, a student has to have the academic record of at least . . . Jared Kushner. Granted, that doesn't leave out many high school seniors, but he was good enough for Harvard after all.

Randomness is inherently fair and has some benefits. There was a rather good Malcolm Gladwell on this topic, but it was not one of his more contagious ideas. He told about a school that selected its student council at random instead of holding elections, with fascinating results. The kids who were picked mostly didn't want to be on the student council, like most kids. And the kids who didn't really want to be there were quite awesome and had innovative ideas. Because most kids are awesome and have innovative ideas. And they got their work done quickly and efficiently, without the usual fuss, because they weren't into student council drama.

There were some intriguing consequences of relying on randomness, which is inherently fair, and most were improvements on the status quo. Pretty interesting stuff, and I think Malcolm Gladwell should leak it again.

You probably think your admissions office is doing an awesome job, because there are amazing young adults running around your campus. But this is a kind of confirmation bias, because young adults are mostly amazing. I should know; they are my life's work.

There might be a range of benefits from adopting a random admissions policy. Some are obvious from the story of the student council. You might get a broader applicant pool, including some people who don't think they can get in with the current system. And you might pick a freshman class that reflects the country, as opposed to reflecting what you are looking for. That would be a good start.

You wouldn't have to worry about pesky courts examining your numbers, because your numbers would be random. Why fight the courts, when you can just *outsmart* them?

But the real benefits would be to the high school students. College rejections would be random, not personal, so they wouldn't find the same emotional purchase. The parenting pandemic might relent, so high school students could enjoy their teenage years, which would set them up for better mental health throughout their lives. And maybe high school students could focus on learning, instead of learning to impress. As any kindergarten teacher will tell you, students who are happy and relaxed learn better. They might even learn who they are.

There might also be less money flowing to the SAT, which is a highly profitable private company with very little social value. And maybe a little of that money could go to paying teachers better. They have extraordinary social value. And they might enjoy their jobs a little more, too. That would be a wonderful side effect.

Some of the benefits would even be for the university. You could shut down the entire admissions office and use those resources to cover mental health services for your students. And maybe if the parenting pandemic and toxic high school culture went away . . . your students wouldn't need so many mental health resources.

But obviously, admitting students randomly would reduce exclusivity and allure. I imagine Harvard sees that as a negative. But I see it as mostly a positive, for the mental health of young people I mean.

So, while I have singled out Malcolm Gladwell as a lab-leaker who sparked a toxic parenting trend, his other idea might offer an interesting solution. At least it's worth thinking about.

Random admissions might have some side effects, like a few bad apples might get through. But it's easy to think of bad apples who have gotten through with the current system. Just take a look at the newspaper.

The Ivy League is probably sitting there wondering how I propose to handle the sports teams. Randomness might admit five hockey goalies one year, and no point guards. There might be too many tennis players or too few football players.

Actually, I have a plan for this.

I think you should drop varsity sports too.

It's time to admit that varsity sports haven't been what you pretend they are for at least a generation. I think you could show leadership on this and say it's time for change. Technically, it wouldn't be showing leadership, because Spelman has already done it. But you guys could just copy Spelman's idea and call it leadership. That tracks.

Sure, there would be a vocal minority bemoaning the end of days, but I believe most Ivy League graduates and faculty would breathe a sigh of relief and say it's about time. Your counseling centers, meanwhile, would throw a party.

But the real benefits would be for youth sports. A generation ago, sports were an important stress reliever for most kids who participated. Now they are yet another stressor for too many kids. Youth sports could be sane again if parents didn't think they were a pathway to elite colleges. And that would be truly great, because sports can be wonderful for kids.

Luckily, the world is going to be a much better place when I am in charge. (Just ask anyone in my office!) Until then, high schools can keep handing out wellness brochures and goop, whatever that is.

CHAPTER TWENTY-FOUR

This Stuff Sounds Serious; Why Is Everyone So Preoccupied with Cell Phones? I Have No Idea—It Honestly Makes Me Kind of Crazy.

The next student is quiet, reserved. Smart, but soft-spoken. Seems depressed, but so far, I'm not sure why he made the appointment. His family moved a lot; his father was a Fortune 500 executive. He went to fancy schools. He went to schools that I have heard of. . . . the kind of schools that thoroughbreds go to . . . he's probably going to have typical parenting pandemic stuff.

He's having sleep problems; that's pretty clear, and that's something I can handle; maybe he needs to think about his priorities a little so he can get to bed earlier . . . no, it's nightmares. This isn't parenting pandemic stuff at all, this is serious child abuse.

More details flow out. It's incoherent, the way traumatic memories always are. There are images that are very clear, but the sequence is hard to follow. He doesn't want to talk about it so he's vague and dodges questions—I have to be quite specific to develop a coherent narrative.

His father got drunk and beat up the entire family on a regular basis.

This went on until he was old enough to ask to go to boarding school for high school.

No one ever did anything. The family moved a lot and lived in wealthy enclaves where people mostly don't know their neighbors. I asked the sort of questions you ask when you're trying to understand how abuse could go undetected for so long. Did he have serious injuries, requiring emergency room visits? Lots of times. His father would go with him and charm the staff. He was an important executive, after all. Did the student show up at school with evidence of injuries? Routinely. Did anyone at school ask about his injuries???

Yes, the fancy schools did ask. Well, that's a relief. But he answered in the way that traumatized children do—he lied. He told the school he was injured playing sports, which his father told him to say, even though he didn't play sports. His father didn't have to tell him to lie; it was unspoken. Children desperately seek the approval of their parents, and will generally lie to protect them, even if they are being abused. *Especially* if they are being abused. Teachers are trained to recognize common features of abuse, such as frequent injuries. But no one wants to see child abuse, so it's easy to accept any other explanation. One of his schools had him meet with a guidance counselor, where he also lied. Of course he lied. An expensive private school wasn't going to believe him anyway. His father was paying the bills.

Secrecy and a power differential—the ingredients of abuse. The more power the perpetrator has, the easier it is to get away with. The more they get away with, the more confident they become, and the worse it gets.

The family was never assessed. The student eventually went to boarding school and grew big enough to fight back. So the abuse has stopped.

But he's still living it every day.

▪ ▪ ▪

She hated her elementary school. The teachers would rank the students on the blackboard every day. Answering a question wrong or speaking out of turn could get your name moved down on the board. But her parents insisted she stay in the school because it was the best school in the region. It would give her the best start in life. *It made her miserable.*

But at least she had piano. She loved it, and it rewarded her. She worked hard and steadily progressed.

She was accepted by a renowned piano teacher in the nearest city. This was an honor. She was overjoyed. Maybe she could leave her toxic school.

The piano teacher sat a little too close to her and touched her hands a lot. She told her parents. They told her not to complain. The lessons were expensive, and prestigious. She had to get used to his teaching style.

She wanted to please her parents, and she wanted to please her teacher. So she didn't complain while the boundary violations increased.

The boundary violations increased.

She stopped practicing the piano. She didn't want to play. Her parents got mad at her for being ungrateful.

She went to college as far away as possible from her parents and the piano teacher. And she immediately stopped playing piano.

▪ ▪ ▪

She's bipolar. She was diagnosed when she was fifteen. But she's not in treatment because . . . she thought she'd be better by now. Her moods are all over the place, and it shows in her grades. Sometimes she does all her work, sometimes she stays in bed.

When did it start? Hard to say. She remembers her mom locking her in the bathroom. Wait, what? To control her moods. Her moods were out of control, so her mom locked her in the bathroom. Um, okay. Is this bipolar or is it trauma?

She loves her parents. She's quite devoted to them. She says she was quite a difficult child. Um, okay, victims of child abuse often blame themselves.

She goes home to see them as often as she can afford.

Medication eventually controls her moods, but there's a lot of evidence of trauma. Now that her moods are more stable, there's time to piece it together.

Young parents, stressed financially, not ready for children. And their child . . . Sounds like their child was difficult, with very stormy moods. They didn't know what to do, or whether it was normal, or how to ask for help. Or what kind of help they needed. So they hoped it would get better.

But it didn't get better, and one day her mom . . . just snapped and couldn't control herself . . . and that's when they started resorting to the bathroom.

And everyone felt bad and she tried to control her moods, but she couldn't, and her mom got more and more frustrated. But by now, they definitely couldn't ask for help, because if anyone knew about the day she lost control, and about resorting to the bathroom lock . . . they wouldn't be able to live as a family. You see, her mom resorted to the bathroom lock because she was afraid she would lose her temper again, but it didn't work perfectly, and every time she lost control, she became more ashamed and swore it wouldn't happen again.

So the situation became more and more secretive, and no one could find out because the stakes were too high . . . and my student still hadn't gotten any help for her mood disorder, which wasn't getting better on its own.

But one day, she trusted a teacher enough to talk about the mood swings. But certainly not the violence or the being locked in the bathroom! And her teacher knew about bipolar disorder and told her where to get help for the mood swings. And she went.

So she got help for the mood swings, but not the violence or the being locked in the bathroom. But the funny thing is, when the mood swings got better, the violence and the being locked in the bathroom also got better. Although the aftermath of those things hung on.

None of this had to happen. If her parents had basic information about normal child behavior and mood disorders, or a nonjudgmental person to go to for support, or even just more help with childcare, this escalating spiral of uncontrolled moods and violent behavior would have been avoided.

This is *intergenerational trauma*. Stressed caregivers, with limited knowledge and resources, who are unaware or mistrustful of the social services available to support families. They don't ask for help because they have had bad experiences themselves or are afraid of being found at fault in some way. They don't believe the system is there to support them, or that it can help them. And through early childhood trauma, the lynchpin of the Big Three, this dynamic can easily be transmitted to the next generation.

Everyone should care about this, because stable environments are optimal for early childhood development. Unstable early childhood environments perpetuate the Big Three. Stable early childhood environments are essential for stable societies.

Luckily for this student, a teacher intervened before it was too late. And this student was able to completely change her trajectory. Lots of other adults helped: the psychiatrist who first diagnosed her bipolar disorder, other teachers in her high school, a guidance counselor, a scholarship program, my office, her professors, her advisor . . . the list goes on and on.

She spent half of her college years working through her trauma, and the other half . . . thriving. Still bipolar, of course, but she has learned to recognize her early warning signs and has good social supports including a strong relationship with her family, and she is managing it well. And she is out in the world now, and she is okay. Now, do some students with this sort of background do okay without all this intervention? Of course! Humans are highly resilient and adaptable. But the deck is stacked.

Her under-resourced urban school did a better job than the fancy school that I've heard of. Changing her trajectory just took one caring teacher with the right kind of knowledge. The fancy school that I've heard of didn't care or didn't look. And this doesn't surprise me, because I see it all the time. To be sure, people everywhere care, especially teachers. It's part of being human. But you only see what you're looking for.

The school that ranks children is even worse. This school is part of the problem. There are reasonable arguments about what schools should and shouldn't be responsible for, but the absolute bare minimum is that schools should not cause trauma. Our piano player's school created the mindset that her achievement was more important than herself, and the dynamic of her parents' prioritizing the authority of the educators over her well-being. Her school set her up for more serious trauma by teaching her to dismiss her instincts, which is extremely dangerous. She was disempowered long before she met her piano teacher, which made her an easy target. Our schools should be helping families raise well-adjusted adults, the kind that work on society's problems and raise well-adjusted children. I'm stating the obvious, and yet . . . here we are.

▪ ▪ ▪

The stories keep coming—sometimes it's more than I can take. Well, almost, but I remind myself it's not me, and it's not happening now, and the person in front of me has already survived and they're likely to recover, at least more or less. And all of that basically works, and I keep it together and act like a doctor.

But sometimes it doesn't work. Sometimes the perpetrator . . . is a doctor.

Yes, more often than I prefer to acknowledge, the perpetrator of the serious abuse that I am hearing about . . . has taken the Hippocratic oath.

When the perpetrator is a doctor, I totally lose my compass. Usually, when I'm lost or uncertain, my default is to ask questions, which almost always helps. But in these cases, the wrong questions come. Didn't they go to med school? Didn't they learn something there? Weren't there pediatricians running around talking about child abuse all the time, and how serious it is? Didn't they have to learn some psychiatry? Didn't they learn that emotions can be powerful, but you can learn to manage them? Don't they care about people? Isn't that why they went to med school? Isn't it obvious how twisted this is? How do they go to work every day? How can humans be so flawed that this is even possible? Are they torturing patients? Is there any hope at all?

This is what being a psychiatrist is like: all day long you listen to stories about the worst things that humans do to each other, frequently within families, and try to help people cope with the aftermath. There are lighter moments to be sure, but in general, at the core of human psychological suffering lies trauma . . . inflicted by other humans.

Then you go home at the end of the day and read newspaper stories about mental health. And the stories are about genetic testing for antidepressants, and fMRI studies, and phones, and new terminology in the diagnostic manual. None of these things helps you understand people, and none of them helps you understand suffering. Sure, there are technical details that might improve diagnostic rigor, or tweaks to some treatments that may impact quality of life a little for a few individuals. But it's like cleaning up the ducks at the edge of an oil slick, while a massive tanker is still leaking.

You cannot substantively improve mental health outcomes without addressing child abuse. You just can't. And no one talks about it. We prefer to talk about genetic testing for antidepressants, and fMRI studies, and phones, and new terminology in the diagnostic manual.

In normal times, the disconnect between how I spend my days and how mental health is generally discussed befuddles me. Year after year after year, I shrug it off and get back to work. But sometimes it bothers me.

In crisis times, it makes my head explode.

▪ ▪ ▪

I think we previously established that some people think I might be a child abuser. Well, at least one person thinks that. Maybe she's retired and I'm off the hook. But I know she is not the only one who has had that thought about me, because the other person who has had that thought . . . is me.

Because I am a human and sometimes have bad days. This happens more often than you may think if you have three children under the age of five, especially if you haven't had your Yo-Yo Ma nap.

So sometimes I have thought that it might be possible to hit a child. Because I have OCD, and it's an intrusive thought, and I need Exposure and Response Prevention? No, because I am a human. I have days when my frustration tolerance is not at its best, and poor frustration tolerance doesn't mix well with toddlers. Especially certain toddlers who think it's funny to kick you in the face with their snow boots while you are buckling them into their car seat.

But it has also come up that I went to a college that sometimes people dream of attending, but that drops you if you become disabled and can't play your sport. And I also went to a famous medical school that does a good job teaching the difference between U-rology and Neu-rology, even though they really do sound the same. And you have also definitely learned by now that there is a kind of doctor called a pediatrician. (Actually, maybe there are a couple of med schools that don't have any pediatricians; that would honestly explain a lot.) Pediatricians do a really good job teaching about child abuse, even though no one really listens because people are too busy and mostly don't want to believe it. Because who would want to believe it?

So on my really bad days, do you know what I do? I do what people with jobs and money do, which is to say, I call my nanny. On her day off. More than once. And she comes right away and gives me a look that is kind, not professional.

I'm pretty sure that no one's goal in life is to become a child abuser. It just doesn't make sense, if you think about it. You meet the love of your life, and you get married and think of the future, and imagine your life . . . as a child abuser? Or you come to this country from far away for the sake of your family to build their future . . . to be a child abuser? Or you go through infertility for years and it's scary and lonely and quite painful . . . to become a child abuser? No, I don't think it's anyone's goal to be a child abuser.

I think it mostly starts small because you're lost and confused and you don't have support, but once you cross a certain line it's hard to go back, and . . .

I think it's a slippery slope.

▪ ▪ ▪

I read a lot of parenting books when my kids were younger. If I were to write a parenting manual, it would be one page long, and this is what it would say:

Don't beat your kids. Or commit child abuse in any of its other forms. And stay far away from child exploitation too, just to be on the safe side.

Have fun with them. Lots of fun. Fun is evolution's way of telling you you're doing it right. Pretend they are puppies, if that helps.

Teach them the value of sleep, and layering. Teach them this over and over again, because they weren't listening. They will forget when they turn thirteen. Then they will blame you for not teaching them.

Teach them to cross the street. Their skills will peak in fifth grade. When they are no longer able to cross the street safely, they are probably ready for college.

When your child turns eighteen, the most important variable in their overall prognosis in adult life is the quality of their relationship with you. Make every parenting decision with this in mind. Hint: I've never spoken to an eighteen-year-old who wished their father pushed them harder, or their mother micromanaged them more.

People need to make their own mistakes, often big ones. People learn more from the consequences of their actions than they learn from nagging parents.

They will forgive you if you don't let them get a ferret, or go bungee jumping, or get a tattoo. Well, definitely yes on the ferret; I'll get back to you about the bungee jumping and tattoo, but I'm pretty sure.

You can't change them, but you can ruin your relationship trying.

Ditch the "achieve at all costs" mentality. It's not worth it.

Show them the joys of exercise but watch your step around youth sports.

But mostly, don't beat your kids.

Oh, and allow fifteen extra minutes in the morning. It really helps.

That's it. I don't think it would sell many copies or do well on the talk show circuit. But it's the truth.

Need help now?

They don't know what your dad was like. If you've had an argument with your teenager, don't expect them to congratulate you for handling it better than your own parents. I'll congratulate you, though! Good job! You deserve a lot of credit!

April—Blunt Forces

CHAPTER TWENTY-FIVE

When the Real World Happens Right Next Door—The Boston Marathon Bombing

If it's April, it must be tax season. Well, I wouldn't know, because one of the many wonderful things about my husband is he is an absolute control freak when it comes to taxes. I haven't done my own taxes in this century, which is a truly wonderful thing. So I will never have to remember when Tax Day is. Except I can never forget when Tax Day is. It's the day of the Boston Marathon bombing.

The Boston Marathon runs through the BU campus, and students throng the course every year. Full disclosure, it's usually a party. It's a holiday, and often one of the first nice days of spring. Let's just say there's a lot of extracurricular activity.

The bombing was a shock to the community. Many students were at the finish line as spectators, as volunteers working the medical tents, and as photographers. Everyone is affected.

One BU student dies.

Our phones are ringing off the hooks. Students need to talk to someone. We triage, we set up groups, we handle as many students as we can. It's too much to manage on our own, and other departments help.

For a week, it was unclear if it was over. There were military vehicles in the streets, which fed the sense that it wasn't. And then there was the lockdown, back before anyone had any experience with lockdowns. Can you go to the grocery store in a lockdown? No. The airport? Yes.

No one knew if we should act normal, or scared. So we did what we always do, which means we took care of the kids.

I spoke with affected students. A lot of them. I have no idea if I said anything helpful or not, but I listened, educated them about the stress response, and discussed coping skills.

A colleague checks in: "How are you doing?" I have no idea; how am I doing? I haven't felt like this since 9/11. That sense that all your patients are going through something terrible, but you're going through the same thing. Trying to help people, while staying above water yourself.

"It feels good to be useful," I answer.

He nods—he has to run. There are calls to be returned. There is a lot of serious trauma.

There are also a lot of broken thumbs. Students who lost a cherished belonging in the chaos or can't get into their home for several days because of police activity. Events canceled and exams failed. Not huge traumas, but real things, especially for young people.

But there's something else, too. Something I am definitely not expecting. A student walks into my office. He has struggled with anxiety for a long time, and we've been working on a number of strategies. He tells me he doesn't need to see me anymore. Because he is better.

"I realized that all the things I worry about aren't real problems. The bombing was real. The things I worry about are mostly things my brain is making up." Almost all my colleagues have a case like this. Perspective is valuable for young people, but the cost is quite high.

You need to help, now.

Be a positive adult for all the teenagers you know. Kids are a package deal—they come with friends. You're not going to like all of them, but you don't get to choose. Many teenagers are somewhat difficult, and a few are downright prickly. If you know a teenager like that, consider this: You might be the only adult in their life who doesn't yell at them on a regular basis. Please be that adult. You might be saving their life.

CHAPTER TWENTY-SIX

When the Real World Happens in Your Office—Pandemic

Something weird is happening. First, it's just a few news stories, about people far away. Then more stories. Closer, but still far away. Our family takes our usual winter ski vacation. I try to keep up with the kids on the mountain. It doesn't go well. I keep up with the news in the early mornings. It's not going well. On the way home, we see a few people wearing masks in the airport. The kids ask why. It's time to tell them.

Things are even weirder at work. One of my students is from Wuhan. She tells me what she's been hearing from home. It's worse than the newspapers are saying.

Time to tell my parents to stay home. I tell them not to go to their activities for a while, or the grocery store, or even church. I tell them not to go to the emergency room unless they think they are dying, because a trip to the emergency room might kill them. My siblings wonder if I'm paranoid. I respond with data. I may or may not be paranoid, but data is just data.

It's BU spring break. The students are mostly away from campus. President Brown announces that classes will be held remotely for a few weeks. The students have to stay home or figure out how to get home from wherever they are. They don't have their stuff. It's total chaos.

The DEA relaxes interstate prescribing rules. I'm suddenly sending prescriptions to every pharmacy in the country. I'll never be able to memorize all their street addresses! How can there be two Walmart pharmacies on the same street in a small city in Alabama? And how can my software be so brainless that it can't find "Walmart" when I type in "wallmart"?

Our department is switching all appointments to zoom. Today. My anxiety about technology . . . talk about exposure therapy. It feels weird at first, but we get used to it. After a while, I can no longer easily remember if I've ever met a given student in person.

Zoom becomes the new normal. But it's not normal. I can't rely on visual cues or intuition. I have to ask more questions. Are you losing weight? Are you getting out of the house? *Are you getting dressed?*

A student suddenly goes silent and stares. Is she hearing voices? Dissociating? Having a seizure? Is her mom talking to her? Did the Zoom connection freeze?

None of the above. There was an earthquake in her location, two time zones away from Boston. An actual earthquake. She's okay. What if she weren't? What would I do? Would I call her emergency contact, probably her mom, and tell her there was an earthquake? She probably knows! So what would I do?

I would probably sit here and feel powerless, *which is what I'm already doing*. I've always been powerless in this role. People come to appointments or not, follow my recommendations or not, and get better or not. So I've always been powerless, but this earthquake, the real one and the metaphor, make me feel utterly ineffectual.

But students keep scheduling appointments, so I keep showing up.

Social distancing. They taught us about this in med school, but it wasn't catchy like "a diet that works" or the U-rology vs. Neu-rology thing. Everyone forgot. Even the few meticulous students who remember the pediatricians screaming about child abuse forgot about social distancing.

It seemed like a dystopian joke. They taught us that social distancing involved closing stadiums and canceling public gatherings, as well as not traveling and severely limiting social interactions. As med students, we comforted ourselves with the knowledge that modern medicine had relegated pandemics to the historians and promptly forgot about social distancing.

But "social distancing" started appearing everywhere, only it wasn't a joke. And now I'm a psychiatrist who spends a good deal of her time trying to get people to spend more time interacting with other humans, and for good reason. *This is going to be a disaster.*

At least it's only for a few weeks.

It probably won't be that bad.

▪ ▪ ▪

Start Zoom meeting.

Are you there . . . Can you hear me?

I can see you—I just can't hear you . . .

Pretty sure it's my Zoom connection—oh no, just need to unmute. Got it.

Now do you hear me?

No . . . what do you hear?

Your mother calling . . .

. . . calling to say she loves you—she does. I know a thing or two about mothers and sons. You see there's this stereotype, and it's one of these stereotypes that is true, and . . .

No—she can't call you—she's gone . . .

She's calling in your head—that's the voice you're hearing. Try listening to my voice . . . I'm a mother . . .

Well, not a good mother—at least not right now. No, he's okay. Actually, he's not okay, but I know he will be eventually. He's home with his father and the '86 Mets, and a rather long Ken Burns documentary as well as several dozen books about baseball, including a whole series by Cal Ripken Jr. . . . who's kind of known for being reliable. He can lend his mother to you for a while—he'll be fine, and you're rather close to the edge, and rather alone. You have all of the Big Three, plus daily drinking, which you like because it allows you to hear her voice for a while, which further increases your risk.

I know she's calling you—she wants you to join her, on the other side. I don't blame her.

Can you stay on my side of the abyss?

Can you borrow me for a while? You can break a piece off if you need to—it grows back. At least, that's what's always happened. And now . . . I actually don't know, but I have more than I need, so you can take some. My son can spare me; he has good prognostic signs, including a father who can step in for a while . . . and you don't. Yours mostly beat you and your mother at whim and had the power and wealth to easily conceal it.

So can you borrow me? I won't hurt you. Come to think of it, I can't even touch you because you're on the other side of a Zoom screen. Good thing you are, because if you were in my office I'd have to resist hugging you, because that's unprofessional.

So will you listen to me instead of her? Try turning up the volume on Zoom.

You're worried about whether you were a good son. But I know something you don't. Being a good son doesn't end when your mom dies. True, I wasn't there; I don't know anything about whether you were a good son in the past . . . but you have the rest of your life to be one.

Well, it seems like you're listening to her, so maybe just look at me. I'm on your computer screen.

Could you lay off the vodka a bit, because it's yet another suicide risk factor?

What's that? You need to hear her right now? Tell you what—can you just listen to her and look at me, and maybe—pretend to listen to me? I pretend to listen to people all the time; I'll tell you how. Get out a piece of paper and start a grocery list. It looks like you're listening. Made you laugh.

I think we'll get through this—not sure myself at the moment, though, no. It's what humans have always done, though the slippery slope has always been there. In your case, it's an abyss. Can you step back a little? It's slippery and you're very near the edge. Just step back a little? It's still a huge abyss, but there's less likelihood of falling. Yeah, now stand there and look at me. That's better.

What's that? Gotta go? See you next time.

End Meeting.

▪ ▪ ▪

What day is it? I don't know.

Is there school today?

Who knows?

Does it matter?

Who knows?

Luckily, it's only for a few weeks. I can survive anything for a few weeks.

What day is it? What month? What season?

Are my parents alive?

Am I?

The grocery store is insane. Out of toilet paper. Out of Diet Coke. Out of Diet Coke for months. Might not survive that.

I feel my colleagues collapsing around me. I hope they can't sense my own uncertainty.

I hear Charlie Baker's voice every day. I'm hearing voices.

No, I'm not; at least I don't think so. It's hard to say anymore. But he's on TV every day. Actually, I just hear soundbites on the radio . . . I don't have time for TV . . . I'm drowning in work. Everyone needs me, and they're pulling me under. It's too much. But I hear Charlie Baker's voice every day. He keeps going, so I guess I can too. At least I can pretend; maybe that will be enough. *Maybe that's what he's doing.*

There's a grown-up in charge . . . at least here.

Charlie, thank you. Good luck at the NCAA. Oh, that reminds me . . . on the topic of the NCAA, I have some ideas about how it could support the mental health needs of athletes. You see, sports are overall good for mental health but there are some real problems . . . you can't just stick young people on sports teams and think your work is done . . . there are power differentials . . . a hotline would help . . . and I think more education about eating disorders is needed. Some recruiting rules need updating. Like maybe if a recruited athlete becomes disabled, the college should have to honor the commitment and accept them. I know, it doesn't seem like a rule like that should be necessary. There's quite a bit to explain. So, I was thinking we could have lunch and discuss the mental health needs of college athletes, and also how NCAA policies trickle down and affect youth sports. And I could thank you for being a grown-up when the world needed it. But be ready to take some notes, Charlie, because your work isn't done.

More challenges—worse than the Diet Coke shortage. My older son has a concussion. It happened at wrestling practice. Don't worry, he'll be better in a few days, just like the pandemic will be over in a few weeks.

Except he won't, just like it won't. He continues to be a zombie. He sits and stares blankly. For hours. He barely moves. He doesn't fiddle with his orthodonture or roll his eyes at his parents. There is nothing more terrifying than a fifteen-year-old who doesn't roll his eyes at his parents.

I ask for more work-from-home days. The office will make it work . . . I don't know how . . . we've lost a quarter of our staff like everyone else . . . basically everyone with a child under the age of five . . . also like everyone else.

So I'll work from home. There's nothing to do for a concussion . . . just wait . . . but it feels better to be nearby. It also feels better to be working, because the time passes more quickly . . . or at least it passes. I wonder if I listened to those patients. I hope I did a good job pretending.

After a week, there's no change. Still no eye rolls or fiddling with orthodonture. I'm scared. I think this is when other people might pray, but—don't tell my parents—I'm an atheist. I don't find comfort in prayer. *Huh, still hanging on approval from my parents.*

No, I find comfort in numbers and statistics. I look up the probability of a complete recovery in a time frame that we haven't reached yet . . . and I find . . . a number that a casino would bet on. The house always wins, so he will get better. He will get better. I just know it.

But I also know he has to stop wrestling. The injury happened in the normal course of the sport—a routine takedown. There was no foul play . . . no rules broken . . . and takedowns are the point of the sport. This will happen again if he continues. A casino would bet on it, and the house always wins. So he has to stop wrestling. So I have to talk to my husband.

And in spite of everything I've learned in a career of dealing with the terrible fallout from concussions . . . I can't believe how hard it is to even bring it up. Wrestling transformed our son from an awkward tween to a confident high school student . . . it kept him focused and connected to others during the worst of the pandemic . . . it was part of his identity . . . and he has to stop. I regretfully think of the parents I have judged for not pulling their children from sports that were destroying their brains or bodies, and I forgive them a little. Actually, not quite forgive, but at least understand.

So it's hard to even bring it up. But the only thing worse than making him stop wrestling is . . . not making him stop wrestling. My husband agrees immediately . . . I don't even get the words out. The only question is how or when to tell our son.

So we just start telling him every day, calmly but clearly: We're pulling you from wrestling. It's not your choice. Your coaches already know. You're not going back. Your job is to get better; our job is to make this decision. There will be other sports, other teams.

We have this conversation at least five days in a row before he remembers that we've had it before.

He never questions our decision, or our prerogative.

▪ ▪ ▪

I keep going. I'm not sure how, but I do. It's just what humans have always done. But some days I'm exhausted, and eventually I run out of helpful things to say. One day, I find myself saying, "If you find yourself in a hole, the first thing you should do is stop digging." Now, this is excellent advice, and you could argue that it sums up CBT. But it's actually a Leo McGarry quote.

You probably remember that I didn't learn anything in residency other than: Don't call your patients because they might think you care, don't make eye contact with patients in public because they might think you are human.

But I did learn a lot from *The West Wing*. It's better known for teaching Gen X that politics can actually help people. (Well, I never believed that because of the counterfactual of . . . all the actual politicians.) But I learned many things that were applicable to mental health. Like lots and lots of Leo McGarry quotes, which are useful to have on hand if you are an exhausted clinician, it turns out. There are many wonderful characters, but Leo definitely has the best repertoire for psychiatrists. Phew!

It doesn't end with Leo's quotes, though. You could base an entire psychotherapy training program on *The West Wing*. Remember our friend

Yo-Yo Ma? He's in it! He is a key figure in a series of episodes that teach quite a bit about trauma. It's well done—the viewer learns about sequelae of trauma such as irritability, avoidance, and substance use, as well as distress at triggers. This was way before everyone was talking about trigger warnings all the time—in fact, the incident that started the whole thing could frankly have used a trigger warning. There was a lot of foreshadowing, which is what we called trigger warnings back then.

There's also a lot on fathers and daughters, which you have already learned is important. You see, President Bartlet has three daughters, and he really loves them, but sometimes there are misunderstandings . . . I'd better back up a bit. Bartlet was president when I was in residency—he beat Al Gore. It was a really close election, and I'm not exactly sure how it happened. (In residency you don't have time to follow both the news and *The West Wing*—you have to pick.) But I'm pretty sure that's how it went, because Gore won the popular vote, but they decided to go with someone who was more dynamic on TV, which is how we got President Bartlet. I think that's how it happened. It was all decided by someone named Chad, but I truly never understood how or why.

Anyway, President Bartlet was a very good father. So good, in fact, that in season four he took a break from being president for a while because worrying about his kidnapped daughter was making him irrational. Spoiler alert! I mean trigger warning! Wait, those are opposites, but here they both apply. Huh. Some people want to be warned and some people don't. Humans. Too complicated to understand.

So President Bartlet worried so much about Zoe that . . . they found her! That's how effective worrying is! Just ask Meghan! Oh sorry, spoiler alert, but in this case no trigger warning applies, so maybe humans aren't completely hopeless after all.

So I learned about fathers and daughters during residency, which has really helped my family life. For example, when my daughter wanted to go to the *Eras* concert, I said, "Go ask your father," and told her to cry a little bit. She thought I was blowing her off, but I knew that any father would bankrupt himself for this, especially if he saw her crying. And that is exactly what happened! He missed a day of work to fight off the bots and pushed back our retirement plan for a year or two . . . all for a concert in the rain! And they were both excited about this outcome! You see? Fathers and daughters are insane!

■ ■ ■

Sometimes students just find their way to the wrong office. A student is here today, near panic. She can't catch her breath, and I have to slow her down with breathing exercises. She says she needs Xanax.

So I talk to her for a while. She's anxious. It's near the end of the semester, and she has a major art project. But that's not the problem. The problem is, she needs five hundred dollars of supplies for the project, and she's out of money for the semester. So she's panicking. And needs Xanax.

"There's no amount of Xanax that's going to make five hundred dollars appear," I say. Actually, that's not true, but we have to keep it legal. I talk to the student about emergency loans and slush funds and send her to the deans' office.

(Also, I give her a Xanax prescription, because panic attacks suck, so maybe she did come to the right office.)

A different student is discussing his major. He's trying to decide whether to write an honors thesis, and is considering the pros and cons. He's been obsessing about the decision, so he thinks he has a mental health problem. I'm assessing him, because he made an appointment, but he seems fine, and I truly can't see where this is going, and I definitely don't know whether he should write an honors thesis.

"I think you should speak with your academic advisor," I say.

He looks shocked. "What should I talk to him about?"

Academic advice?

We are going to stay with these two cases for a minute, because they illustrate some important things that I would like you to understand. These two students came to see me because they were having strong emotions, not mental health problems. There's a difference. (You could argue that it's more of a continuum.) Think of an iceberg, where the tip represents mental health problems, and the bulk of the iceberg represents the range of human emotion. To some degree, an individual can move up or down the iceberg, toward the tip or away from it. From what you have learned about the Big Three and important life events around age twelve, certain people are at higher risk of remaining near the tip more of the time. But in our office, we see many young people who think they have a mental health problem but are just experiencing a normal emotion.

Let's talk about what emotions are for. They are not random, and they are not weaknesses. Emotions are highly evolved shortcuts that help us navigate our environment, just like our physical senses. What do I mean? Take your sense of touch. If you are making s'mores by a campfire, and your hand gets a little too close, your body pulls it away before you get burned. You realize your hand is hot after you have already pulled it away. The circuits that control this action are very well described, but what you need to know is that your cortex, the thinking part of your brain, doesn't have to get involved. This is good, because for the purpose of avoiding getting burned, your cortex is too slow. For the most part, people don't get burned making s'mores by a campfire.

Your emotions are like that. They tell you something is wrong, to motivate you to do something. Like the student who needed money: She didn't know how to solve her problem and needed help getting money, but she kept ignoring her anxiety signal until it got worse. Or the guy whose worrying was telling him he needed academic advice; he thought his worrying was the problem, but it was just a signal. And remember our friend the philosophy major? Many people get to the point of needing to see a mental health clinician because they have been *ignoring* their emotions, instead of paying attention.

Let's go back to our campfire example for a second. Imagine if we taught children who were standing too close to the fire to ignore the physical discomfort and press on making a perfect s'more for their dad. Obviously, we'd have a lot more campfire burns. But we'd also have children growing up with a lot of confusion about how to keep their bodies safe from basic dangers that they are highly evolved to avoid.

There is another trend that I find a little troubling. In general, the message is out there that people should seek mental health support if they are struggling. But some people interpret that to mean anyone with any strong emotion should be in therapy. There are a couple of problems with this. First, it pathologizes a normal state, because emotions are mostly normal.

Second, it deprives people of a chance to deepen their relationships in the real world. If you cry to your friend about a breakup, it is good for both of you. You feel better, because you have cried and talked to someone who cares about you. Your friend feels better, because they have been able to help you, and helping others has enormous mental health benefits. And you both benefit from a closer friendship, which further enhances your resilience, and your self perception that you can get through difficult things. These things are profoundly important. If you go to a therapist instead, it reinforces the idea that emotions are mostly pathological and meant to be experienced in confidential places, and that you can't get through difficult things without a professional. This is not healthy for you, and it's not healthy for society.

There is another reason why it is problematic if too many people go to mental health clinics for normal emotions, and this brings us back to the Covid pandemic for a moment. You have probably heard that college counseling centers were totally overwhelmed during the pandemic, not to mention the entire mental health system. *Relatively benign cases like these two students were a big part of it.*

During the pandemic, just about everyone experienced some emotional fallout, and slipped down their own slope at least a little. Mental health problems became more acute, strong emotions became mental health problems, and normal emotions became strong emotions. So everyone felt a little out of sorts, and a whole lot of people decided to deal with this by seeking mental health support in some form.

The whole iceberg floated a little higher, so the new tip of the iceberg was huge. Still, most of the cases were relatively mild. In our office, we have a very effective screening system. We were able to identify milder cases and refer them out, so we would continue to have capacity for the more serious cases coming in. Remember, preexisting mental health problems became more serious, so we did have a much higher level of acuity than is normal for us, but we never turned any serious cases away. Some people were mad about being referred out, for sure. If you are isolated and struggling and your boyfriend broke up with you, it is a small comfort that other people have it worse. But we are a finite resource, and this is what we had to do.

In the general community, it was far worse. In this country, there is no organized system for mental health care, just a haphazard web of clinics and private practices. During the pandemic, all these practices were flooded with new patients, for the same reason that my office was. Providers did the best they could, but there was no systemic way of ensuring that the most acute cases were able to get into treatment. Worse, because you really had to persist to get a therapy appointment during this time, for the most part the openings that became available went to people who persisted the most, which is to say, people who were already well-resourced. All of these factors, combined with the fact that numerous mental health clinicians left the field or cut back on their hours because they were also stressed, led to the near collapse of mental health care during the pandemic.

There was no particular cause of the mental health pandemic; it was death by a thousand cuts.

May—Graduation Requirements

CHAPTER TWENTY-SEVEN

How to Promote Mental Health: Individual Factors

I don't know if I can say any of the things in this book. The closer I get to the truth, or at least my truth, the more I think I am saying something you are not allowed to say.

I am holding people responsible. I am holding individuals responsible for themselves. I am holding parents responsible for their children. And I am holding everyone responsible for their communities. I'm not sure if I'm allowed to do this. But what else is there?

Because if you make an appointment with a mental health provider, what you are going to find is . . . a person. A person with ears and time, which quite frankly everyone else has too. And if a mental health provider offers you something much more complicated than ears and time, I would frankly be somewhat skeptical. Because you are a person, too.

It's fashionable to talk about mental health like it's mysterious, difficult to understand, and outside your control. People prefer answers that seem complicated and modern.

But for most people, mental health is just how you live your life every day. How much sleep did you get? How much physical activity? What did you put in your body? Did you laugh and sing and dance? Did you take care of others? Did you engage in work that was meaningful to you? Were you self-critical, or self-accepting?

The answers in mental health are not found in diagnostic manuals or six-week clinical trials or spreadsheets. They are not found in a bottle of

Xanax or a bottle of vodka or a bottle of Diet Mountain Dew. They are not found in laws or policies. They are not found in public outrage, or newspaper articles.

In mental health, the answers are mostly found in taking care of yourself, taking care of your family, especially children, and taking care of your community, especially children.

Help others. Evolution rewarded helpfulness because groups with more prosocial behavior procreated more successfully and survived better. So helping is part of a lifestyle that is optimal for mental health. If it takes more than a paragraph to describe how your work is helping others, it's probably not. Do something else.

And be kinder. Just about all of us could work on this one, including me. (That's probably obvious!) If more people were kinder than they have to be, and fewer people were fanning the flames of outrage, things might get a little better. I really think so. And it's worth trying, because the first person who might benefit . . . is you. Because mental health isn't only about the things other people do to you. It is about the things that you choose to do yourself.

Sleep more. If you are reading this book, you are probably not sleeping enough. This is not my opinion—it's science. Well, it's my opinion too. But research shows that contemporary humans are sleeping fewer hours than at any time in history. In fact, if current trends continue, in another fifty years humans won't be sleeping at all.

Seriously! Just look at the graphs! Graphs don't lie! Now, this is going to put an enormous strain on the global caffeine supply chain. The coffee growers will be totally overwhelmed. I am obviously already hoarding Diet Coke, and I am not planning to share. Everyone else is going to have to resort to Diet Mountain Dew.

When most of humanity resorts to drinking copious quantities of Diet Mountain Dew to get through their sleepless lives, it is going to create a huge problem for mental health professionals like me. Everyone will walk into my office carrying a two-liter bottle of Diet Mountain Dew! How am I going to diagnose eating disorders? How will I differentiate between a student with anorexia and a student surviving life on no sleep? I will have to learn the diagnostic criteria for anorexia! And imagine how many times the arugula-eating experts in meetings will change the criteria over the next fifty years! How on earth will I keep up?

So please, sleep more, so I can stop imagining this dystopian Diet Mountain Dew future! It's making me so anxious that . . . oh no, that's another diagnosis that I might have to develop a new shortcut for!

I have a couple of easy techniques for assessing sleep deprivation in the office. The first is to ask about sleep latency. This is a useful term, referring to the amount of time it takes to fall asleep after turning in. It's common for a college student with a sleep latency of ten minutes or more to report insomnia. But normal sleep latency is fifteen to thirty minutes. Sleep latency less than fifteen minutes suggests sleep deprivation. Less than five minutes suggests serious sleep deprivation. Most college students I meet guess that five minutes is normal sleep latency.

I am going to say this in a different way, because this is really important. The amount of time it takes to fall asleep that most college students consider normal is suggestive of *serious sleep deprivation.*

Another simple technique for assessing sleep deprivation is to ask how difficult it is for an individual to wake up in the morning. So high tech! (Do not try this at home, people! I am a trained professional!) If a person is generally well-rested and on a consistent sleep schedule, they should wake up before their alarm about half of the time. So I commonly ask college students how often they wake up before their alarm.

You should see the reactions I get; they're honestly priceless. Imagine a child approaching random strangers at the park and asking if they have been to Mars lately. Some adults would probably laugh or give a quizzical look. Others would clutch their purse a little tighter. But many would politely explain to the child that travel to Mars is impossible.

That's right. Many students I meet don't seem to understand that it's possible to wake spontaneously in the morning. Some swear that they have never done so. They explain that they have always been woken by an alarm, a roommate, or a parent. They believe it's not possible to wake up on their own.

I love it when this happens.

You have gotten to know me by now, so you are probably already imagining how much fun I have when someone earnestly tells me that it's not possible for them to wake spontaneously. What do I do? I ask questions, of course! I have a lot of great questions for a situation like this!

I start by asking about any recent vacations, and whether they really set alarms every day. Then I ask what they do when they're ill and have to stay in bed all day. Do they wake for meals? What about trips to the bathroom? I ask about when they were younger. Did they ever sneak a TV show before school? Did their mom wake them for that, really?

How do they suppose their mom wakes up? How did people wake up before electricity and alarm clocks? What if everyone was asleep at the same time, and there was no one to wake everyone else up? How do they suppose infants make their parents miserable? Do parents get up at two in the morning to wake their babies and make them cry, so they can then complain to the world about their infant crying all night?

I could go on like this all day. From what we have discussed about learning and repetition, you have probably guessed that the reason I could go on like this so easily is that I have had this conversation many, many times. There are a lot of people who don't believe that waking up in the morning is a normal process, because they have to be woken by something external. This is a sign of severe sleep deprivation, but they think it's normal.

And then they wonder why they're tired all the time. Seriously.

It's not normal for a healthy adult to be tired all the time! You don't have to go to med school for that, people!

Adequate rest is one of the most important determinants of mental health at any age, not to mention a host of medical problems. Modern humans are not sleeping enough.

Exercise more. Preferably outside, like your ancestors. It can't be coincidence that so many cultures developed religious traditions that begin with long pilgrimages. But any exercise will do. Physical activity helps just about every problem that I commonly deal with.

Want proof? Go to your local marathon or 5K and ask the participants how they are feeling as they cross the finish line. (Do this carefully, or you may end up with your microphone or various body fluids shoved in your face.) You will get a range of responses, but I guarantee not one runner will tell you they are feeling anxious or depressed.

So exercise more. How much? The American Heart Association says thirty minutes three times a week. If it's good enough for them, it's good enough for me.

Okay, I obviously made that up. I have no idea what the American Heart Association says these days, but I say that all the time. Thirty minutes three times a week *sounds* good, and it's not very intimidating, so that's where I usually start. If that's pretty easy for you, then gradually work your way up toward an hour a day. Somewhere between the American Heart Association and Barack Obama is probably right for most people.

How vigorously? A lot of ink is spilled on this one. There are fancy gadgets that cost hundreds of dollars and can give you continuous feedback on the intensity of your workout. The newspapers publish lengthy articles on the various pros and cons of these gadgets, which coincidentally have very large marketing budgets.

So how do you determine the right level of exercise intensity to achieve mental health benefits? Here's what I tell BU students: If you can easily sing the Happy Birthday song while you're doing it, it probably doesn't count.

Put yourself on a news diet. I think most people should not expose themselves to the news for more than thirty minutes a day. That's right—the old Walter Cronkite model. That's enough for most people to understand the issues of the day, and I think more than that is . . . mostly bad for you. The news only talks about the bad things that happen, so if you follow it obsessively, you will start to think only bad things are happening.

It's like asking Meghan if I am a good psychiatrist. Good grief! Whatever you do, do not ask Meghan if I am a good psychiatrist!!! She will probably tell you that half of my patients were hospitalized over the weekend!!! That would be a disaster. No, if you want to find out whether I'm a good psychiatrist, just ask one of the many people whom I told to sleep more, or prescribed Xanax so they could fly home for Thanksgiving. Honestly, you can ask just about anyone other than Meghan!

Remember what you have learned from CBT. Thinking about bad things makes you feel bad, which makes you think about bad things . . . So the more time you spend thinking about the news, the worse you will feel.

Are humans evolved to be able to withstand stressful events? Of course! Humans have survived a remarkable number of challenges, as individuals and as a species. We have a highly evolved stress response that provides energy and motivation and resourcefulness to survive a severe event, like a crop failure or maybe a conflict with another band of humans. But the stress response has a cost—it is not healthy over the long term. In the course of normal events, a community of humans probably encountered a major crisis every so often. A healthy stress response helped them survive. The stress response resolved after they survived the event.

In modern life, most communities don't have a major crisis every year. But there is always a crisis somewhere, and the technology exists to monitor every crisis closely. Your brain doesn't know the difference between a crisis here and a crisis somewhere else and may go into a stress response about something far away that is beyond your control and doesn't directly impact your life. And if you do this repeatedly, it can cause a chronic stress response, which is bad for you. Chronically, an unresolved stress response can cause a range of medical and mental health problems.

So put yourself on a news diet; you'll be glad you did. Besides, you're not likely to find the solutions to the mental health crisis there. The newspaper's job is to keep you reading the newspaper, not to find solutions.

And while you're at it, stop blaming everything on Mark Zuckerberg . . . well, the mental health crisis, at least. This will be easier once you stop reading the newspaper so much, since blaming Zuckerberg is their default mode.

Come to think of it, you *can* hold Zuckerberg responsible for the mental health of children, but only three of them. That's right, he has three daughters, just like President Bartlet. The role of parents is extremely important in mental health, and I think that Mark Zuckerberg . . . I think he is probably an excellent father.

Bet you didn't see that one coming! Actually, I didn't either. It's kind of like our famous coach, whom my husband and the media consider a jerk, but I know to be a good father. In the case of Zuckerberg, there are some good signs. First, his children are not household names, and none of them shares a name with a popular consumer product (that's a very low bar, I know, but that's the world we live in, people). Keeping children out of public life in today's world is extremely important, so the fact that he is doing so is a very good sign. Next, his wife is a pediatrician, so . . . that kind of speaks for itself. She's probably not letting the girls do gymnastics.

But the main reason I think he is probably a good father is that he was raised in quite a stable family, and his own parents are still married. These are huge predictors of psychological well-being, and therefore huge predictors of how a person will handle the stresses of parenting. And to top it all off, I just learned (you are going to love this one!) that his mother is a psychiatrist! Way to go, Mark, you just won father of the year!

You see Mark, I do hold you responsible for the mental health of children, but only your own. And between the pediatrician and the psychiatrist, I'd say you have awesome guardrails. If they're not around and you're not sure how to handle something, just remember that children are like puppies. You won't go wrong.

And Mark, if you choose to use some of your resources to buy Taylor Swift tickets, I will totally respect that. If you don't want to go to the concert . . . I have a suggestion . . . just hire a babysitter. I know this teenager, and she's really good with younger kids, and she's only seen Taylor Swift live twice, which apparently isn't enough . . . just a suggestion.

Oh, and Mark, in case it wasn't clear, I don't recommend a private all girls' school.

That's all, Mark; see you at the next reunion. Oh yeah, you didn't actually graduate, but don't worry about that . . . Harvard will take anyone . . . if the price is right.

Listen to more Taylor Swift songs. You saw that one coming, right? I was a little late to the party on this one, but I have been listening to a lot of Taylor Swift lately, and my mental health is awesome! I know, you're thinking I'm the maddest woman, but my mental health is excellent. That's right!

The only diagnosis I currently meet criteria for is multiple personality disorder, and that diagnosis—no longer exists! So I have a clean bill of health. I definitely don't meet criteria for an anxiety disorder; we have established that.

I wish I had been more familiar with Taylor Swift during the pandemic, because she really would have helped me out. There is literally a song for every emotional scenario, so when I totally ran out of things to say . . . instead of quoting Leo McGarry, I could've discussed a T. Swift song. Or maybe even just played one. That would've been so much easier!

I love quite a few of her songs. There's some real wisdom there about taking care of yourself emotionally. Such as, sometimes you need to let yourself be sad for a while; it opens the door to moving on. Sometimes you should own your mistakes. Things that are worth doing generally involve significant emotional investment. The importance of friendship. And if someone hurts you, you can really stick it to them with a song.

This gives me an awesome idea. Now, Taylor, I don't think you went to college. (Seems like the sort of thing a normal author would just look up, but there you have it.) But if you had gone to BU, you probably would've been classmates with my colleague and AOC (also born in 1989), which honestly sounds like a lot of fun. Anyway, you know quite a bit about human nature. Stay away from Shakespeare; human nature is the purview of important anonymous people who write diagnostic manuals. Kidding of course. (If you do write a song about diagnostic manuals, make it a song about stuff you'd like to burn.) But did you know Shakespeare has some new stuff out? There's been quite a bit since *Romeo and Juliet*. There are lots of plays, and some poetry, too—he's really prolific, like you. Also like you, he's inspired by his exes; he had this really intense relationship with Gwyneth Paltrow in the late nineties, and . . . I'm not sure if that's how it happened. I was busy being a med student at the time, so I didn't keep up with pop culture all too well, I mean all that well. But anyway, check out some of his other stuff!

Getting back to my point, you know a lot about human nature, so it won't surprise you to hear that many colleges have a problem with sexual assault on campus. This issue is discussed a lot, so you may assume things have improved in the past generation or so. Let me quickly summarize the progress that has been made since Gen X was in college to bring you up to speed.

Zero.

Huh. That was pretty easy.

Well, technically, there's been some progress in certain areas, and other things have gotten worse, and honestly everyone seems much more confused, so it all averages out to zero progress.

Here's where you fit in. When someone is accused of sexual assault, instead of judicial procedures and slaps on the wrist, or criminal charges that get dropped for "lack of evidence," . . . instead of all that . . . you just write a song about them! Here's how it could go. You just have a few songs prepared with a blank space. When a sexual assault occurs, you just add the name to the pre-arranged lyrics that fit the situation best . . . and then—justice and retribution, T. Swift style! Actually, I don't think you'd even have to write any songs. If potential perpetrators knew you were planning this, they would behave themselves. Men are terrified of your songs! Because a Taylor Swift song is forever and always.

Oh, Taylor? One last thing. You see, quite a few Swifties have started families, and they could honestly use some new lullabies, and I was thinking . . . for your next collaboration . . . a really good idea would be Yo-Yo Ma. I don't know if it would be popular . . . that's not really my expertise . . . but I do think working with Yo-Yo Ma would be really good for . . . your mental health.

CHAPTER TWENTY-EIGHT

How to Promote Mental Health: Family and Societal Factors

Practice intergenerational un-trauma. That's right! You've learned about intergenerational trauma, which is bad, but there's also intergenerational un-trauma, which is good. Most people don't know about intergenerational un-trauma, because if you have it, you're mostly fine, and therefore don't need to think about it.

Remember when Tolstoy said all happy families are alike? This is what he's talking about. Intergenerational un-trauma is not the stuff of thousand-page novels. It's honestly quite boring. And mostly people don't even know when they're doing it, or if it's making a difference.

Happily, intergenerational un-trauma is not at all difficult. You don't even need an advanced degree. How do you do it in real life? You may have guessed that in our family, part of intergenerational un-trauma is skiing. I skied with my family of origin when I was growing up, and I taught my own children to ski. (I made them learn on a rope tow.) My husband didn't really ski when we met, but he saw that skiing was important to me. He is an individual who is willing to try new things, and he made an effort; these things are also part of intergenerational un-trauma.

Well, obviously we don't ski you-know-where, because we don't want to be crashed into by people who can't see, I mean ski.

Now, some people consider skiing to be a waste of resources, and I understand that position. However, I think tight-knit families are extremely important, plus skiing is fun, so to me it's spending resources. However, I think we can agree that the thousands of outdoor hot tubs at Deer Valley are mostly wasting resources.

It's not just skiing; there's lots of other intergenerational un-trauma. We like hiking and doing puzzles. Lately, I particularly enjoy watching our younger son beat my husband at chess—now that is quality entertainment. There's also cooking and eating, lots of reading and walking the dog, and once a year on Christmas we . . . Actually, we don't go to church on Christmas because years of working in mental health have turned me into an atheist. But last I checked, atheists can celebrate Christmas if they want to.

Well, that's not all it's turned me into. I'm also a communist because of the poverty and a libertarian because of the arbitrary prescribing rules, and . . . I guess working in mental health has turned me into a person of contradictions. Which is to say, a human.

But for many people, religion is a very important part of intergenerational un-trauma, so keep it up if that's your thing, it's just not mine. But I do celebrate Christmas, so go figure. This intergenerational stuff is . . . kind of hard to break.

In other words, intergenerational un-trauma is mostly just doing things you enjoy with people you care about. This is obvious, because it makes you happy, which is evolution's way of telling you . . . it's a very good idea.

But it's not just about your own family. (If you only have the energy for your own family that's completely fine with me, because if you do a good job with intergenerational un-trauma, your child will never need to come meet me, which will honestly free up time in my schedule. I know, I sound so charming and personable, but it's honestly just better not to meet me.) But if you are able, you can do a tremendous amount of un-trauma in your community. For example, you can start a robotics team, or take kids hiking, or host Dungeons & Dragons.

Or you can coach soccer, which I did for many years. Well, *coaching* is the strongest possible word for what I did. It would be more accurate to say I spent quite a bit of quality time with a group of awesome girls who were mostly doing cartwheels while I was mostly fighting off a toxic competitive culture, all the while looking for opportunities to discuss child exploitation. And we had a blast!

Whether just in your family or in your local community, intergenerational un-trauma is fun and benefits everyone involved, but you mostly don't know when it's happening. If you are lucky enough to live in a community like mine—well, apart from the potholes and the rats—it happens quite a bit. But some communities don't have enough—you probably know that—and you should support organizations that are trying to change this.

Think you don't need to worry about all this? Think you can insulate yourself from intergenerational trauma? Think it doesn't affect everyone? Think again. Let's go back to the thoroughbreds for a moment.

First, I have to pause to give Prince Harry a trigger warning. Harry (I hope you didn't mind being called a mustang; seemed like the sort of thing you wouldn't mind)—okay if I use your first name? I'm unhappy about the way the media in my country covers your estranged family.

Harry, since we're talking, would it be okay if I come give you a hug? It would help me resolve something. You see, early in the pandemic there was this young man whose mother had just died, and his father's family was treating him terribly. And she was calling to him from the other side, and he was quite close to the abyss, and I wanted to jump through the Zoom screen and hug him. But I couldn't because the technology hadn't been perfected—or at least I didn't know how to use it—and because of professional boundaries. And now I know he's alive, but I can't go find him and give him a hug because that would be totally creepy, and still a violation of professional boundaries. But he took one of my starfish arms, and it hasn't healed, and I haven't moved on.

But I could come give you a hug, because your mother died, and your father's family treated you terribly . . . and when I read your book you reminded me of him. And I wouldn't presume, but your mom—well, your mom never would have agreed to be played by Gwyneth Paltrow in a movie; I think we can agree on that. But it might have . . . sort of . . . worked, except for the skiing thing—I hear your mom was more of a Lindsey Vonn. You see, I have two boys of my own, and I know about mothers and sons. I have no sense of fashion (that should be clear by now), so there's that, but I'm a bit of a Lindsey Vonn myself. I have scars for sure . . . but I'm strong from all the regrowth . . . and maybe if your mother had lived to be a grandmother to your children, she'd look a bit . . . Well, she'd probably have some scars and be quite strong.

So, if I dropped by and gave you a hug it might help me resolve this, and I think . . . maybe you wouldn't mind either.

After we hug and cry a little, or even quite a bit, we could have lunch with your Meghan and talk about dogs and whether the name Meghan should have an *h*, which is a topic of considerable controversy in my office.

Okay, that sounds fun, but I'd actually like to talk to you about your work with veterans. You may recall that I mostly didn't learn anything in residency, but that is not completely true. I learned quite a bit about trauma from working at the VA. Who would've thought it? Not me—I didn't realize I was learning, because I was going home at 5 P.M. every day, and you can't possibly learn anything if you're not stressed out and exhausted. (Huh, I'll have to ask a teacher about that.) Anyway, this experience led to a lifelong interest in veterans as well as the origins of my understanding of the importance of early childhood trauma. So we can also talk about that. And I know of a couple of veterans' organizations you may find interesting. So, let's talk!

But back to your family, I truly do not understand the newspaper coverage of your family in this country, up to and including the most prestigious outlets. You see, funny story, my ancestors fought a war against your ancestors, and—spoiler alert—my guys won. I know! They probably didn't teach you that at Eton, but it's true! So, to me, your dad is just a guy with a rather obscene welfare check, who honestly could have used social services to help with his parenting.

How did a man with such extraordinary privilege become such a terrible father? Does wealth make you a bad parent? No—ask Mark Zuckerberg; he just won father of the year. The answer is intergenerational trauma.

Closed doors and power differentials create the opportunity for abuse, and castles have both in spades. I think your father was abusive and neglectful because his father was—that's more or less how it works. And the story of your family is an illustration of how difficult it is to break the cycle of intergenerational trauma, even with all the resources in the world. No one is immune from trauma, not even kings.

For us to function better as a society—from mental health to improving our courts to addiction to achievement gaps—it is essential for everyone to understand trauma better.

Get a dog. You probably guessed that one. I'm writing after the pandemic, so you probably followed this advice already. In my neighborhood, there are lots of dogs, and lots of happy families. Dogs love you no matter what, whereas humans have competing demands. For kids, dogs have all the qualities of a perfect parent—always waiting at home, reading their mood correctly, and not asking much in return. For parents, dogs have all the qualities of a perfect child—they're happy to see you, they do what you say, and they don't talk back.

How do dogs do this? They are capable of near perfect empathic attunement. Remember empathic attunement? It's why your dog is your dog, and not just an animal living in your house. It's also why it's possible to fall in love with someone who doesn't speak your language or communicate with a preverbal toddler. And it's why your dog will always be a better companion than an AI.

Dogs are the perfect family glue. When your children go off to college, they're not going to care about seeing you over Thanksgiving, but they're going to be eager to come home and see the family dog. I can practically guarantee it.

Universal preschool. Wow, that came out of left field. Is she serious? Yes, actually—I think it would help a lot. Preschool is wonderful—it builds friendships for children and communities for the parents. And all families, rich or poor, can benefit from taking a break from each other. It encourages healthy boundaries.

Not to mention preschool teachers have a wealth of experience helping young children develop emotional regulation, while most modern parents frankly don't. So yes, I think universal preschool would help. Early childhood development is too important to leave to chance.

And while we're being serious, how about taking on income inequality? The parenting pandemic didn't start in a vacuum, and Malcolm Gladwell doesn't get all the blame. Parents are legitimately terrified about what it means for their kids if they fall behind. It doesn't have to be that way. Scandinavian countries have the best mental health in the world, and it's not because of the hot chocolate. It's the social safety net.

Stop child abuse. There is no way to significantly improve mental health in this country without solving the problem of child abuse. Child abuse leads to severe mental health problems, and it is the lynchpin of intergenerational trauma. The pediatricians are right about child abuse. It's everywhere, and you have to look for it constantly. We can't leave it to the pediatricians and teachers.

Solving the problem of child abuse is like splitting the atom.

Honestly, one of the reasons it's so hard to solve is that people are mostly unaware of it. Just like atoms. Yup, they exist! And they're literally everywhere! But, spoiler alert, we split the atom! We seriously did it! Well, not me personally, but some very smart people, and . . . Actually, this has been done quite a few times. There was a very popular movie recently, all about how handsome nuclear physicists usually are, so you can just watch the movie. But we did it. And nuclear physics is incredibly complex, so surely, we can solve a problem as simple as . . . human behavior.

Oh dear; I think I'm going to have to start over.

Okay, I guess we need a more modest approach. Let's tackle it like Obama took on health care. Maybe our first attempt won't be perfect, but it will be a good start . . . so whoever comes next can build on what's working and make improvements. Oh wait, it didn't happen that way. Forget I said anything.

But you have to start somewhere, just like you have to start exercising or composting or writing a book. I'd say the best way to start is to just . . . start!

I think the easiest place to start is to not commit child abuse yourself. And stay with me for a second, because if everyone took this step, we wouldn't need to do anything else! Problem solved!

If you have been paying attention to this book you may have noticed that being a parent is full of challenges and frustrations, and caregivers could honestly use more support, so a great next step would be to support anyone in your life who takes care of children. And by support, I don't mean saying, "I support you," though that could be part of it. I mean giving them a break from parenting when it's needed and giving them honest feedback when that's needed.

Even rich families need a lot of help, so if you know a family just . . . help! Helping people is easy, because all you need is your ears and time, and all you do is ask what someone needs, or maybe just notice. If helping is unfamiliar or uncomfortable or feels like overstepping, just get your hands dirty, pretend your name is Mitzi, and help! You won't regret it, because the secret of helping is . . . it makes you feel good.

And be a part of your community. Voting a certain way or donating to charities is not enough, although those things would also be great. Everyone needs to be paying attention. Know the names of the children in your community. Be an approachable, neutral adult. Ask questions about injuries, or absences from school. The worst that will happen is that they will think you care about them.

Stop talking about stranger danger. This just teaches people to be afraid of each other, when what's needed is stronger communities. Children need to learn to *calibrate* relationships, recognize red flags, and set boundaries. They need to learn this in all kinds of relationships, and they can only do this by interacting with people. Remember that most abuse occurs between people who know each other well. On the other hand, health care providers and emergency responders are usually strangers. The message of stranger danger is confusing and unhelpful.

Listen to children and take them seriously. Teach them to trust their instincts. That sounds complicated, but it's actually easy because all you have to do is listen to them and take them seriously.

Remember the ingredients of abuse: a power differential plus secrecy. With children, there's always a power differential, so there can never be secrecy. Be very suspicious of secrets. There's a possible carveout for surprise parties, but in general children should learn as early as possible that there are no healthy secrets.

Abuse is shrouded in secrecy. There's no screening tool that is going to find it. A victim will never tell someone they don't trust.

Remember that the public persona of an abuser is not what you think. It's not the surly coach whom everyone considers a jerk—he's often a lovely father behind closed doors. Abusers can be quite charming and charismatic and exist in all walks of society. They sometimes pay a lot of money for fancy schools or hold positions of considerable power. You can't make assumptions.

Identifying child abusers is tricky. We have systems in place to trigger mandatory assessments in certain situations, which may or may not be productive. If you have been paying attention you may recall that . . . I was once more or less accused of child abuse. Which is to say I was assessed, which is different from accused . . . except it doesn't feel different. It feels like something you wouldn't wish on your worst enemy. And because of what you have learned about emotional memory, I remember it really well.

Well, it was over a decade ago, so I don't remember most of it. I have a hazy recollection of the kind pediatricians who knew about accidents. The only person I remember clearly is the one who made me cry. Because crying makes you remember things. That's the entire basis of CBT. And if someone makes you cry on one of the worst days of your life, you remember it, and maybe even go through life a little afraid of people who resemble them, even though it's irrational.

But you may also have noticed that I am someone who is familiar with the bathrooms at Deer Valley, with their gold-plated toilets. And bathrooms are confidential, like my office. If a person who knows about gold-plated toilets at Deer Valley has one slight brush with the system and remembers it over a decade later because she cried that day, there might just be something wrong with the system.

Child abuse usually starts small and is relatively easy to deal with in its early phases. But people have to feel comfortable asking for help, and this requires *trust*. And as long as the system that exists to support families is the same one that takes children away from families, I don't think trust is possible. We can't have a system in which people are afraid to ask for help. It's literally never going to work. This is an epic problem, even worse than Epic. So I do think structural changes are needed.

Struggling families don't need jails or courts or judgment. Struggling families need help. But they won't ask for help if they think they're going to get jails or courts or judgment.

You're not off the hook if you just sit there and say structural changes are needed. Do all the other stuff too. This problem requires everyone. And probably some structural changes.

Actually, I have no idea how to solve the problem of child abuse. If it were easy, we would have done it by now. Well, hopefully, anyway. But I don't think the answers are in laws and policies and systems. I think the answers are in shared humanity and loving communities and people paying attention and supporting families . . . and maybe a few puppies.

Need help now?

Trust them. I know, that sounds insane. I call it "radical trust," because it doesn't come naturally. But for nearly two decades, college students' biggest complaint about their parents has been, "They don't trust me." So steel yourself and trust them. There's also a practical problem: If you're not going to trust them, anyway, they have no incentive to behave in a manner worthy of your trust.

CHAPTER TWENTY-NINE
Graduation Week

Graduation week. It comes faster every year, and it's already here again. A student is sitting across from me, uncertain what to say. We both feel a combination of relief and disbelief.

"I didn't think I'd make it to this point," she says.

Me neither. I've seen tons of students struggle to the finish line; it comes with the territory.

But we both know it's not the graduating that was in question; it's the being. She's alive, and neither of us were sure if she would be. But here we are—graduation week.

"How do I thank you?"

Oh no—the most dreaded question. There are no good answers. There are several bad ones, though, so I probably throw out one of those, like: "You thank me by enjoying your life," or "by doing meaningful work and contributing to the world," or (the worst possible answer) "by paying it forward." Cringe. You'd think I'd have an answer by now, but I just don't.

So I make my cringe-worthy response, and we both notice how awkward it sounds, but neither of us cares. Because that's where the magic lies. Being an imperfect human and being comfortable with it. Self-acceptance. That's the biggest gift I can give them, but it only works if I personify it.

Luckily, I make plenty of mistakes, so there are plenty of opportunities to model self-acceptance.

She asks for a hug. I can't say for sure if I gave her one or not, because that would definitely violate professional boundaries. But maybe I forgot that rule on this particular day, or maybe I just decided that it didn't apply to someone who wasn't sure if she would live to graduate but did.

▪ ▪ ▪

A department has asked our director to discuss the mental health needs of students at a faculty meeting. She asks for volunteers. And this department . . . well this department is particularly notorious for having a high number of mental health crises. So, of course, I volunteer even though it's usually my work-from-home day. I want to tell them about all the things that contribute to mental health, like not pushing children too hard, and protecting them. And I want to tell them about sleep being as important as breathing, and the thing about Bank of America, and of course Yo-Yo Ma.

And . . . I obviously have to start with the Big Three, because otherwise they'll never understand how everything else fits in. And also, how poverty affects college students more than most people think. And I'm definitely going to have to explain the parenting pandemic, though a group of professors is probably going to understand it right away. University professors have been the essential workers.

I'll probably mention that they can stop worrying about phones. They will be secretly relieved because they all find their phones really useful.

But they have a topic they want to discuss. And their topic is important, but I also know you can't talk about mental health by talking about just one topic, so I will obviously have to explain everything else. I want to say something quippy and memorable like, "If you're not seriously talking about the Big Three, you're not talking seriously about mental health." But the Big Three isn't even a real thing. It's just something I made up to help other people understand that while mental health is complicated, you won't get lost if you keep in mind a few basic principles. So I will have to explain that too.

But there are several of us going, and the faculty will want to speak too, because that's probably what faculty do in meetings. So, in the best possible scenario, I will have about five minutes in which I can say . . . about as much as you can say in a newspaper article.

And I have too much to say for a newspaper article.

I have so much to say—well, I have so much to say that I . . .

I could fill a book with it.

POSTSCRIPT

To my patients, if you see yourself in these pages, it is probably because I cared about you, because that's what sixty-five million years of mammalian evolution have built me to do. When we were working together, I didn't know that I would write a book, or that you would be in it. But your story stuck with me, because it has something to teach to someone in the future, who might be struggling like you were. Or better yet, to prevent someone from struggling like you were.

And to my patients, if you don't see yourself in these pages, it is probably because I cared about you. But I thought your story was unique and so impossible to tell in a way that maintains privacy while still retaining its truth. Or I thought the university's lawyers would be uncomfortable with it. Or maybe both. Or perhaps not enough time has passed for me to understand what you taught me. Or I just miss you and want to keep your story to myself. Or maybe all those things.

I know that when you decided to come to BU, you weren't dreaming of meeting someone like me. But I'm awfully glad you did.

IN CASE OF EMERGENCY

The National Suicide & Crisis Lifeline is available 24/7/365. Call, text, or chat **988** for a confidential conversation.